The Christmas Craft Book

Thomas Berger

The Christmas Craft Book

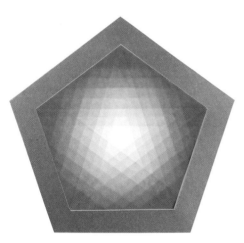

Floris Books

Translated by Polly Lawson

Translated by Polly Lawson
Photographs by Frits Dijkhof
Illustrations by Ronald Heuninck

First published in Dutch under the title *Kerstversieringen*
by Christofoor Publishers in 1990
First published in English in 1990 by Floris Books
Reprinted in 1991, 1993

British Library CIP available

ISBN 0-86315-110-8

Printed in the Netherlands

Contents

Foreword

Of all the festivals which we celebrate in the course of the year Christmas has a special place. Once, many years ago, at the darkest and coldest time of the year a shining host of angels appeared to shepherds in the fields to herald the birth of the long awaited Saviour. Through this event the whole of life upon earth has been profoundly changed.

This is the festival of the light that came to earth, the festival of the birth of the child Jesus. This is the festival which we celebrate afresh each year, which requires so much preparation, especially with children in the family, lest it come upon us all too suddenly.

The inner preparation for Christmas is best begun at the end of November or the beginning of December; that is, at the beginning of Advent, for Advent is the time of expectation and preparation. Some people actually celebrate Christmas during Advent by buying a Christmas tree early in December, decorating it immediately and lighting it. This is regrettable, since children are thereby deprived of Advent, which ought to lead them gradually to the great festival of light.

This book contains many Christmas decorations which you can make with children. By occupying ourselves and children in making these things, we create an atmosphere of preparation and expectation which fosters the spirit of Christmas in the soul of the child. In addition to various Advent calendars and motifs from the Gospel story, other Christmas elements are included: lanterns with their intimate light, transparencies through which the light can shine, folded transparent stars with their pattern of rays, and straw stars which irradiate a warm light through their smooth, golden-coloured surface. Also included are a number of three-dimensional figures, for the world of form and numbers also belongs to Christmas.

Few of the Christmas decorations contained in this book are original; they have been made in countless variations for years. By collecting them together, and by showing how a decoration can be developed by making a very small modification, we hope to encourage you to try things out and develop your own variations.

A word of thanks is due here to the many people who have contributed to this book. Only a few have been named in the list of contents, but many parents of the children of the Vrije School in Zeist have helped with the making of Christmas decorations for this book.

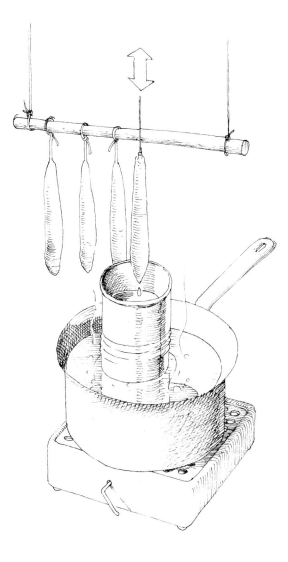

Figure 1. Dipping candles.

1. Candles

Dipped candles

Materials
Beeswax or candle stubs
Candle wick or a thick cotton yarn
Tall narrow tins
A saucepan of hot water
A hotplate or spirit-stove

Method
Dipping candles requires much patience. Put some water in a saucepan to boil. Put the bits of wax or candle-stubs in a tall narrow tin, and put the tin into the saucepan of heating water to melt the wax. The depth of the wax in the tin will determine the maximum length of the candles. When the wax has melted, the saucepan can be transferred to a hotplate or spirit-stove on the table. Lay some newspaper underneath to catch any spilt candle-grease. Keep topping up the water to replace what has evaporated. Wax takes a long time to melt and as it then slowly solidifies on the hotplate it is a good idea to have a second tin of melted wax ready to hand.

For the wick cut a length of candle wick or cotton yarn long enough to prevent children getting their fingers into the hot wax. Before dipping pull the wick taut with both hands so that the finished candle will be straight. Dip the wick into the hot wax for a moment, draw it out again and allow the wax on it to set before dipping the wick in again. In this way a new layer is added each time. At the base of the candle a blob of wax will form and grow bigger each time the candle is dipped. Cut this blob off with a knife from time to time.

Once the candle is finished leave it to cool and harden. This can take several hours, so it is a good idea to hang the candle up by the wick to prevent it being damaged.

The hot water and the wax are *very* hot! Young children should only dip candles under adult supervision.

Decorated candles

Materials
A thick candle
Candle decorating wax in various colours
A thick knitting-needle or a spatula

Method
As shown on Figure 2 candles can be decorated using various techniques. In each case the wax must first be made workable. Take small pieces and knead them well until the wax has become warm and soft. The simplest method of decorating candles is to stick little bits of coloured wax on to the candle and then work them into shape. You can use a spatula or knitting-needle to shape the finer details. New colours can be made by thoroughly kneading two different

coloured bits of wax together (as for example red and yellow making orange).

Make sure that the coloured wax is properly warmed when you press it on to the candle otherwise it will not stick on properly and may come unstuck later.

Decorating candles by smearing

Materials
A thick candle (off-white or white)
A piece of fine sandpaper
Candle decorating wax in various colours
A thick knitting-needle or a spatula

Method
Use a piece of fine sandpaper to roughen the place on the candle where you wish to place the decoration. Warm a small piece of beeswax between your fingers beginning with the lightest colour. Press a little bit of beeswax on to the candle and smear it out very thinly with your warm fingers to give a transparent effect. Now layer the darker colours carefully over the lighter ones. Use a knitting-needle or a spatula to define the details; by scratching the wax or by pulling it up you can make forms in relief.

Kneading different colours together for a long time will produce new colours.

The colours black, white, gold and silver are not transparent and so are less used in this method.

This technique requires some practice, but does give a special effect to the candle.

◁ *Figure 2. Decorated candles.*

Clay candlesticks

Materials
Clay
A candle
Water-colours and paintbrush
Transparent varnish
Sprigs of green

Method
During Advent, modelling can be a wonderful occupation. It is particularly appropriate to make candlesticks which can have a great variety of shapes. The candlestick can have a geometric form such as a cube, or it can be an

Figure 3. Clay candlesticks.

angel carrying a candle between her two wings, and so on. The candlestick should have a little saucer to catch the candle-grease which otherwise might drip on to the table or on to your clothes.

Make the candlestick out of one piece so that you do not have any bits of clay stuck on. These often come unstuck when the candlestick dries.

Although you can make the candle-hole to take a particular candle, you must take the candle out of the hole while the clay is still wet because it contracts while drying and so can split if the candle is left in.

Decorate the candlestick: you can stick sprigs of fir, holly, gold-painted acorns, etc. in the clay while it is still soft, and in this way it becomes a Christmas table decoration. Make sure that the sprigs are not too close to the candle flame.

Allow the candlestick to dry out thoroughly and then you can paint it with water-colours. Once the water-colours are dry the candlestick can be varnished.

2. Advent calendars

Advent begins on the fourth Sunday before Christmas and lasts till Christmas itself. If Christmas Eve is on a Saturday, the first Sunday in Advent will fall already on November 27, and Advent lasts four full weeks. If Christmas Eve is on a Sunday the first Sunday in Advent will fall on December 3, and the fourth Sunday of Advent coincides with Christmas Eve. Before you make an Advent calendar count the number of days in Advent.

There are many kinds of Advent calendars. The best known are those in which a child opens one door for each day of Advent. Advent calendars are important in preparing children for Christmas, enabling them to count the days, even in some versions, making visible the approach of Christmas. Advent is the festival of expectation. The colour blue can be seen to express expectation, so it is a colour appropriate for Advent.

An Advent ladder

Materials
A piece of blue cardstock about 10″ × 14″ (25 × 35 cm)
2 wooden slats about ¼″ × ¼″ and 12¼″ long (7 × 7 × 310 mm)
Gold cardstock or cardboard
Gold paper for the stars
Rose-coloured beeswax
Half a walnut shell
A little teased sheep's wool
Glue

Method
Round off the top corners of the blue card. Sandpaper the slats till they are smooth and stick them to the middle of the blue card about ³/₈″ (1 cm) from the bottom and 2³/₈″ (6 cm) apart.

Cut two long struts ³/₈″ (1 cm) wide and 12¼″ (31 cm) long, and as many golden rungs 2¾″ × ³/₁₆″ (7 × 0.4 cm) from the gold card as there are days in Advent including the first Sunday of Advent and Christmas Eve.

Before sticking on the rungs, mark their places on the wooden slats — the distance between each rung should be about ½″ (13 mm). Stick the rungs on, starting at the top and working down. Once all the rungs are firmly glued on, stick the gold card struts on to the slats so that they cover the rung-ends. Round off the tops of the struts which project beyond the slats.

Model the figure of a baby from beeswax so that it can lodge between the rungs. It is advisable to make the child all of one piece rather than making limbs separately and then attaching them. Place the walnut shell with a little sheep's wool in it at the bottom of the ladder for the crib.

From the gold paper cut out as many stars as there are days in Advent. Each day the children can stick a star on the blue sky behind the ladder as the Child descends a rung. On Christmas Day the Child lies in the crib while behind him there is a sky full of stars,

Figure 4. An Advent ladder.

Star-ribbon

Materials
4 ft (130 cm) dark blue ribbon ¾″ (2 cm) wide
Silver cardstock or cardboard
Gold cardstock or cardboard
Straws
Fine gold thread
Glue

Method
Ribbon and a number of stars make a kind of stairway down which an angel can come. Each Advent Sunday is marked by a straw star and the six days between are marked by a silver star; the ladder therefore begins with the first straw star. As with the Advent ladder, count the number of days in Advent for the year. Stars should be made for the right number of days.

The construction of straw stars is fully described on page 36 and a there is a pattern for a five-pointed star on page 81.

First lay out the straw stars and the silver card stars beside the ribbon to ensure that the distance between the stars is roughly the same. Stick all the stars to the ribbon, making sure that you only glue the middle of the star so that the points are not stuck down.

Finally, cut out an angel from the gold card. Beginning on the first Sunday of Advent, the angel comes down one step each day, lodging behind the stars neatly, because the points of the stars are not stuck down.

If you choose, you can place a crib at the bottom of the ribbon, or you can hang the ribbon above the stable where at Christmas the Child will be born.

Advent walnut chain

Materials
As many walnuts as there are days in Advent
Gold paint
3–4 yards (metres) of red or blue ribbon ¾" (2 cm) wide
Small presents to put in the nutshells
Glue

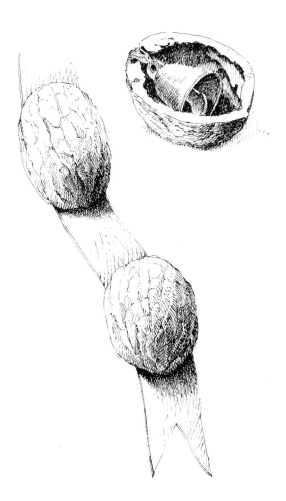

Figure 5. An Advent walnut chain.

Open the nuts carefully so as not to crack or break the shells. Remove the kernel. Keep the two halves of each nut together so that they do not get muddled up.

Paint the outside of the nuts gold and leave them to dry. In one half of each nut place a small present such as a little bell, a dwarf, a shell, a little sheep, a hare of teased sheep's wool, a little stone, a little lump of soft beeswax, a marble, a gold-foil star, a dried flower, a bead, and so on.

Apply a little glue to each half and stick them together with the ribbon running through the two halves.

During Advent a nut is cut off the ribbon each day and opened.

A starry sky as Advent calendar

Materials
A big sheet of dark blue construction paper or
    cardstock
Gold paper for the stars
Glue
A pair of scissors

Method
Round off corners of the blue card to indicate the vault of heaven. Place the card in a suitable place, pin it to the wall, or it can form the background to a tableau for a Christmas crib.

Each day one child, or every child in the family, is allowed to stick a star in the sky. In this way you will have a glorious starry sky as a background to the Christmas crib. Older children can cut the stars out themselves.

3. Wreaths and Christmas table-decorations

Advent wreath

Materials
Thick wire ($^1/_{16}$", 2 mm) for the hoop
Thin wire ($^1/_{32}$", 1 mm) for the candle-holders
Sprigs of green fir
Waxed thread or string
Four candles
A blue ribbon

Figure 6. An Advent wreath.

15

Figure 7. Making an Advent wreath.

in this way so that the wreath gradually increases in thickness, but after the first round use smaller sprigs which are less stiff and more easily bound on. For the last round use short beautiful sprigs to give a smooth and even effect.

For each of the four candle-holders take a piece of thin wire and wind it several times round the bottom of a candle and then bend the two ends down (Figure 8).

Place the candle-holders on four points of the wreath making sure that they do not disappear into the greenery but remain visible. Bend the protruding ends of wire round the bottom of the wreath.

Cut the blue ribbon in two equal lengths. Tie the ends of both ribbons on to the wreath midway between the candles so that the Advent wreath can be suspended by them. The blue ribbon can be wound around the wreath as a decoration if it is not to be suspended.

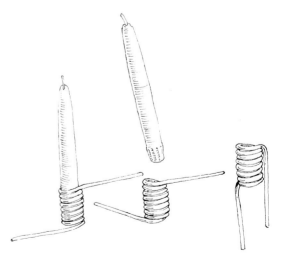

Figure 8. The candle holders of the Advent wreath.

Method

Take a piece of thick wire the length of which is more than twice the circumference of the Advent wreath, to make a double hoop (Figure 7). Twist the ends firmly together. This is the frame and is ready to be covered with greenery. Start by making a foundation with larger twigs, 8″–10″ (20–25 cm). Lay the bottom of the first stem against the hoop and bind it on with the waxed thread or fine string. Lay the next twig underneath the first so that it is overlapped by the first like a roof-tile and bind it on. Continue

A simple door wreath

Materials
Waxed thread or a spool with string
Green fir sprigs
Coniferous greenery
Wire (³/₆₄", 1.5 mm)
Various kinds of evergreen for decoration such
    as holly, coniferous greenery, sprigs of
    spruce fir, ivy, berries, pine and larch-
    cones, lichen, etc.

Method
Make a ring of wire about 10" (25 cm) in
diameter, twisting the ends firmly together
(Figure 7). First attach some rather larger (8"–

Figure 9. A door wreath.

10", 20–25 cm long) fir twigs to make the frame
a bit firmer — as described for the Advent
wreath. Use plenty of greenery and pull the
wire tight. Avoid protruding twigs. After the
foundation of fir twigs continue with coniferous
greenery until the wreath has been built up
evenly all round.

Now the wreath can be decorated using the
wire for support. Any parts of the wire still
visible should be covered.

The sprigs of greenery should not be too big
and should be evenly distributed over the
whole wreath, and arranged so that they
overlap. Give particular attention to the blend
of colours.

To attach pine-cones, larch-cones, berries
and lichen, wind a 6" (15 cm) piece of wire
under the lowest row of scales on the cone. Pull
the wire tight and twist it round a few times with
a pair of pliers. Lichen can also be attached in
this way with wire.

Finally tie a coloured ribbon to the wreath by
which it can be suspended.

Christmas table decoration

Materials
A shallow dish, tin or box containing florist's
    flower block (also called oasis)
Fir twigs for the foundation
Coniferous greenery, preferably fuzzy
Various kinds of leaf: holly, ivy and skimmia
Red berries (not orange firethorn)
Pine or larch-cones on wire (see foregoing)
Lichen on wire (see foregoing)

17

Method
Shape the florist's flower block generously so that it will sit tightly in the box and will protrude. Soak the block in water for about 10 minutes. It can also be secured with two strips of water-resistant adhesive tape (Figure 10). Round off the edge of the block.

Figure 11. A finished table decoration.

Stick fir twigs about 4″ (10 cm) long into the block, slanting downwards, so that the container becomes less visible. Then stick sprigs of evergreen into the block at an angle in the form of a spiral. Keep on going round so that everything is evenly distributed. The sprigs at the top can be a bit shorter than the others.

Avoid using many varieties of leaf or the arrangement will lack harmony.

Finish off with a few sprigs of skimmia with red flowers, holly berries, lichen or pine-cones on wire. You can also insert a candle into the block.

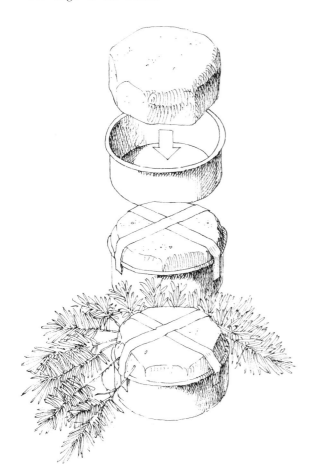

Figure 10. Making a table decoration.

18

Figure 12. A pine-cone wreath.

Pine-cone wreath

Materials
7 pine-cones of the same size
Thin wire
A length of ribbon
A pair of pliers

Method
Make sure that the seven pine-cones are properly dry so that they are well opened. Lay the cones out in a circle and measure a length of wire 2¹/₂ times the circumference of the circle of cones. Bend the wire double making an eye at the bend by twisting the wire round several times (Figure 13). The eye is to suspend the wreath. The length of twisted wire between the

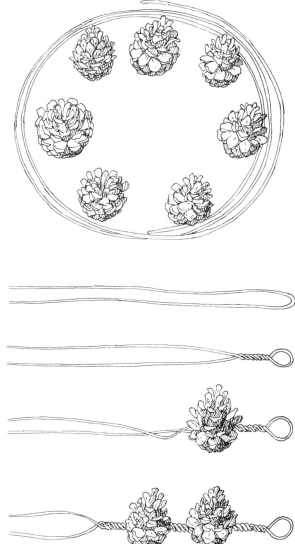

Figure 13. Making a pine-cone wreath.

19

eye and the first cone should be about ³/₈″ (1 cm).

Push the wire between the scales of the first cone about a quarter of the way up from the bottom, twist the wire a few times so that the pine-cone sits firmly between the wires. Attach the other cones in the same way making sure that you twist the wire sufficiently between each cone so that the cones are not too close together, otherwise you will not be able to bend the wire round to make a wreath.

Once all seven pine-cones have been attached bend the whole thing round to make a wreath. Twist the end of the wire a few times round the eye and cut off. Finish off the wreath by tying a bow with the ribbon under the eye. You could also tie in some greenery.

4. Lanterns

A simple lantern

Materials
1 sheet of thin drawing-paper (120 gsm, 32 lb bond)
Water-colours and brush
Salad oil
Glue
A wide jam pot
A candle

Method
The lantern consists of a loose cuff of paper placed over the jam pot (Figure 14). Wet the paper, lay it on a board and smooth it out by wiping a wet sponge over it. Colour the wet paper with water-colours. You should not attempt to paint a picture, but rather try to give expression to a mood with the colours.

Allow the paper to dry and then cut it to the right size. The depth of the paper should be slightly more (but not more than ³/₈″, 1 cm) than the height of the glass. The length of the paper should be about ³/₄″ (2 cm) more than the circumference of the glass.

Oil both sides of the paper sparingly with salad oil. Glue the ends of the paper together to make a cylinder which will fit easily over the glass jar.

Place a night-light or a small candle in the jar and the lantern is finished.

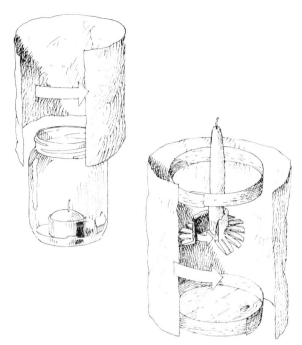

Figures 14 and 15. A simple lantern and cheese-box lantern.

Variation

Instead of the jar you can use a round Camembert cheese-box. Cut away half of the (usually high) rim and remove the top of the lid. Glue the upper and lower rims and stick the painted paper first to the bottom half and then on to the top half of the cheese-box. Finally glue the vertical edges of the paper together (Figure 15).

Take a strip of aluminium foil, fold it several times, and wrap it round a small candle, so that it extends below the candle. Make several cuts in the foil so that it can be spread open in rays and glue them to the bottom of the lantern.

Glass jar lantern

Materials
A large glass jar (2 quarts, 2 litre)
Tissue-paper in various colours
A piece of gold cardstock or cardboard
An old cloth
Wallpaper glue
A sharp knife or a needle

Method
Glue a layer of white tissue-paper around the outside of the jar. It does not need to be smooth all over. The white tissue-paper forms the basis of the transparency.

Refer to the lantern in Figure 16 as a pattern.

Figure 16. A glass jar lantern.

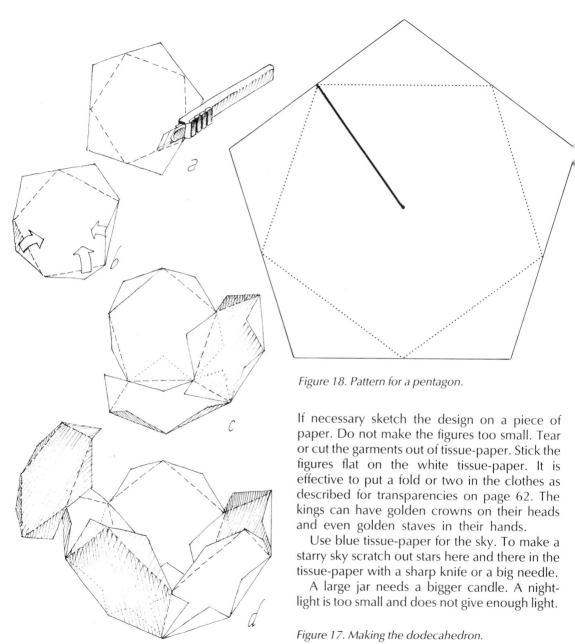

Figure 18. Pattern for a pentagon.

If necessary sketch the design on a piece of paper. Do not make the figures too small. Tear or cut the garments out of tissue-paper. Stick the figures flat on the white tissue-paper. It is effective to put a fold or two in the clothes as described for transparencies on page 62. The kings can have golden crowns on their heads and even golden staves in their hands.

Use blue tissue-paper for the sky. To make a starry sky scratch out stars here and there in the tissue-paper with a sharp knife or a big needle.

A large jar needs a bigger candle. A night-light is too small and does not give enough light.

Figure 17. Making the dodecahedron.

A star lantern

Materials
Thin but strong drawing-paper (160 gsm, 42 lb
  bond)
A pair of compasses or a protractor
A ruler
A knife
A night-light
A glue-stick

Method
This lantern requires eleven pentagons. There
are instructions on page 80 for the geometrical

Figure 19. The starry dodecahedron lantern.

construction of a pentagon. A suitable length for
the sides is about 2½" (6 cm); this requires the
radius of the construction circle to be about 2"
(5 cm). Alternatively use the pattern of Figure
18.

Paint the paper with water-colours before
drawing the pentagons and cutting them out.
Bisect all the sides of the pentagons. Join these
points together, scratching along the lines carefully with a knife. Fold over the triangles thus
obtained to make a smaller pentagon (Figures
17a, 17b).

Now stick the pentagons together in such a
way that the flaps — the folded corners —
always overlap the adjoining pentagon (Figure
17c). As you can see in Figure 17d the best
method is first to construct the bottom half from
the base and then build up the upper edge by
sticking the pentagons point downward on to
the bottom half. On the top edge the flaps are
stuck inside; do the same at the bottom if you
do not wish to have a base; without a base the
candle or night-light is more easily lit.

When the candle is lit inside the five-star
lantern a five-pointed star becomes visible in
every pentagon (Figure 19).

A lantern in the form of a dodecahedron

Materials
Strong drawing-paper (160 gsm, 42 lb bond)
A pair of compasses or protractor
A ruler
A knife
A glue-stick

Figure 20. Pattern for an open half of a dodecahedron.

In construction this lantern looks very like the star lantern, but without the five-pointed stars. Make smaller pentagons with sides of 2″ (5 cm). The radius of the construction circle (see page 80) is about 1¾″ (4 cm).

When sticking the pentagons together, fold the flaps inwards and glue them to each other. In this way they are invisible when the light shines through. The manner in which the pentagons of the top and bottom halves fit together can be seen in Figure 20. There is a pattern on page 82. Stick the top half together in the same way as the bottom half (Figure 21).

This lantern too can be painted before drawing and cutting out the pentagons or can be covered with tissue-paper (Figure 22). If desired the base can be left out as with the star lantern.

Figure 22. The painted dodecahedron lantern.

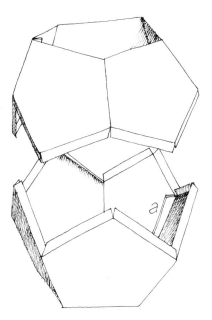

Figure 21. Sticking together the two halves of a dodecahedron.

24

5. Angels

Woollen angel

Materials
Teased sheep's wool, about 18" (45 cm) in
   length
Thin gold or silver thread

Method
When working with teased sheep's wool do not
cut it but pull it apart.
   Separate off one third of the wool for the
arms and wings of the angel.

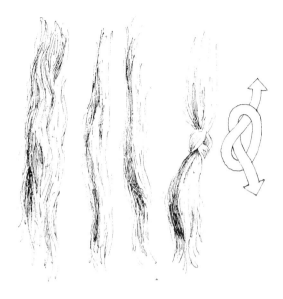

Figure 24. Making the face of a woollen angel.

Figure 23. A woollen angel.

Tie a knot in the middle of the thicker skein
and pull it tight. This beçomes the face (Figure
24).
   Hold the skein vertically letting the wool
above the knot fall down. Spread this wool
round the head as hair and secure at the neck
with a long gold thread. Tie the ends of the gold
thread together to make a loop for suspending
the figure (Figures 25a–b).
   Lay the angel face down. Take the wool
which you have just brought down for hair and
divide it into three parts. Bring the middle part
back up over the head, bring the other two
parts to the sides — they will shortly become
the wings (Figure 25c).
   For one of the arms separate off a bit of wool
about 6" (15 cm) long from the thin skein. Twist
the wool firmly together in the middle, fold the

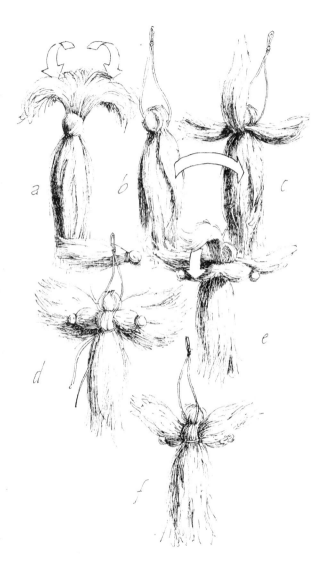

skein double and tie up the hand with gold thread (Figure 25d). Do not cut off the fluff forming the arms. Make the other arm in the same way.

With the angel still face downwards, place the arms under the neck (Figure 25e) and bring the tuft of wool which you laid over the head fall down over the arms. Turn the angel over, push the arms and wings well up, and tie up the body firmly under the arms with a length of gold thread. Allow the ends to hang down as tassels from the belt.

Fluff the wings and robe into shape by holding the wool firmly in one hand and teasing it out carefully with the other.

Angel-mobile

Materials
White tissue-paper
Teased sheep's wool
Gold thread
White yarn
Silvered filigree wire or fine wire
A walnut shell
White beeswax
Glue
A pair of scissors
A pair of pliers

Method
Cut out two square pieces 7″ × 7″ (18 × 18 cm) from the tissue-paper. Lay one of the two squares shiny side down on the table with one of the corners pointing away from you. Fold the

Figure 25. Making the rest of the woollen angel.

26

left and right corners 1″ (2.5 cm) inwards and put a blob of wool the size of a big marble in the middle of the square (Figure 27). Fold the paper over the blob so that the two opposite corners meet, shape it and tie off the head with a white thread. Make hands out of the two corners of the paper and tie them up with a white thread. Give the angel shape, making the upper part billow out so that she really appears to sweep through the air.

Take two 8″ (20 cm) lengths of gold thread and tie one to each hand. Tie the other ends of the two threads together and glue them to the rim of the walnut shell. Take care that the threads are of equal length. Make a second angel in the same way and glue the threads to the other side of the walnut. Cut a length of 6¾″

Figure 26. An angel-mobile.

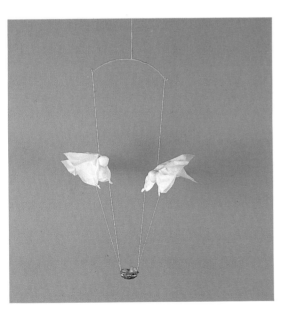

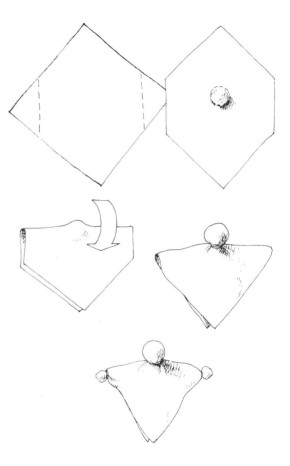

Figure 27. Folding the tissue-paper angel

(17 cm) from the filigree wire and with the pliers bend back both ends of the wire to make loops. Bend the wire to make a slight bow. Tie a gold thread about 6¾″ (17 cm) long round the neck of both angels, this is important for the equilibrium of the mobile. Tie these threads to the loops of the filigree wire. Tie a gold thread to

27

the middle of the filigree wire to suspend the mobile.

Stuff a tuft of wool into the walnut shell (which can be painted gold) and lay a little beeswax child in it. Now the angels can bear the child down from heaven to the earth.

You could make the angels separately or extend the mobile with more angels.

An angel made of gold foil

Materials
White tissue-paper
Teased sheep's wool
Gold foil
A blunt needle or fine knitting-needle
Glue

Method
Cut a square piece of tissue-paper 4″ × 4″ (10 × 10 cm) for the head. Using a little ball of teased sheep's wool make the square into a little head as described for the angel-mobile (page 27). Tie the head at the neck with thread (Figure 28).

Cut out the pieces for the body, arms and wings (Figure 30) by laying the gold foil with the outside uppermost on a base that is not too hard, for example on a piece of soft cardboard, and drawing the forms on the foil with a large blunt needle or a fine knitting-needle.

Attach the head by placing the neck inside the body and sticking the two edges of the body together to make a kind of funnel (Figure 28). Stick the arms to both sides of the body, and the wings to the back. Take a little tuft of teased sheep's wool, spread this round the head for hair and glue it on. Finally make two little hands of tissue-paper and stick these to the arms.

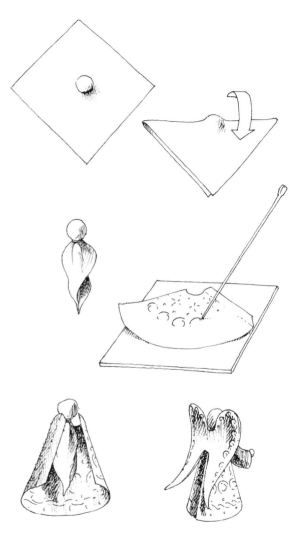

Figure 28. Making the gold foil angel.

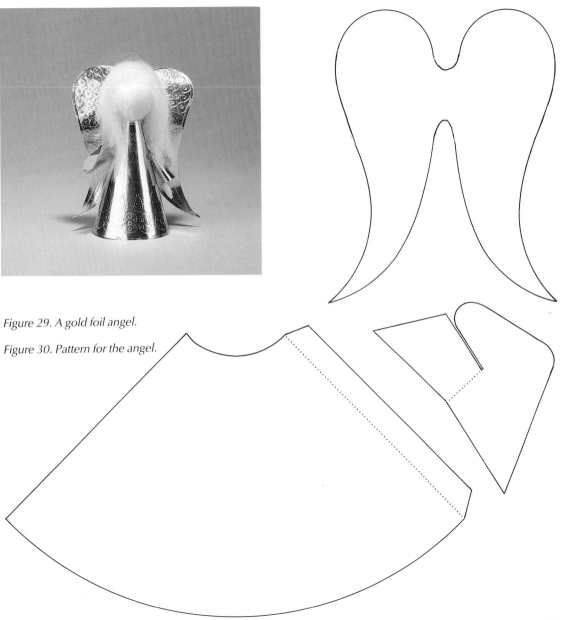

Figure 29. A gold foil angel.

Figure 30. Pattern for the angel.

A straw angel

Materials
Straws
Strong thread or gold thread
Adhesive tape
A piece of gold foil
Glue
A pair of scissors

Method
See page 36 for various ways of preparing the straws.

For the head and body take about eight unironed round straws and allow them to soak in a basin of water for some hours to make them

Figure 31. A straw angel.

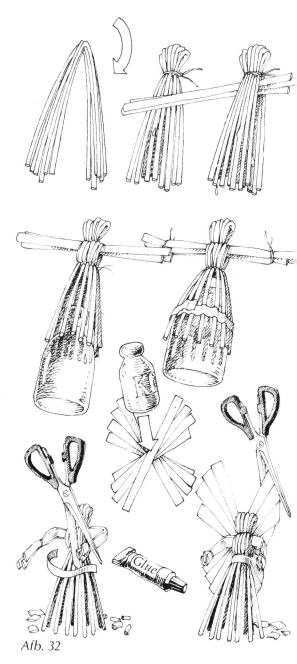

Afb. 32

more pliant. Bend the straws over in the middle. - The length of the halved straws now makes up the head, body and lower half of the angel. Tie off the head with a strong thread (Figure 32).

Take three or four straws which have been ironed but not cut open, and insert them between the round straws of the body to form the arms. Tie off the body. Now try to form the straws which make up the lower part of the angel into a round bell-shape using something round with a diameter of about ³/₄" (1.5–2 cm) — for example a little medicine bottle or a candle — inserting it into the bottom of the bell of straws, so that the straws, which are still wet, are made to stand out. Stick the straws on to the medicine bottle with adhesive tape that can be removed easily afterwards. Allow the wet straws to dry overnight in this position and next day remove the tape. The straws will now form a round bell. Trim the bottom with scissors, but do not cut too much off. Test whether the angel will stand properly by placing her on the table.

While the angel's body is drying you can make the wings. For this take straws which are cut open and ironed flat. Select some good whole straws of approximately the same colour. Lay them across each other in a fan-shape (Figure 32) and glue. Allow them to dry under pressure, so that the crossing place is as flat as possible. You can use adhesive tape here also to keep the wings in shape. In Figure 31 eight straws are used for the wings.

When the angel's body has dried and the lower part has been trimmed you can finish off the arms. Glue the arm straws together and bend them forward before the glue dries. At this point these straws have not yet been trimmed and the angel has very long arms. In fact you can now tie these arms together with a bit of string to hold them in front (Figure 32). Once the glue is completely dry trim the arms to the proper length and make hands by tying the ends of the straws together with a thread.

Before attaching the wings dress the angel. The angel in Figure 31 has a girdle made of a strip of gold foil. You can also give the angel two golden bands crossed over the breast and a golden headband which can have a star.

The fan of ironed straws will become the wings. Glue the fan on to the back of the angel's body. When the glue is dry clip the wings to the correct shape.

The number of straws determines the thickness of the angel, but do not use less than eight straws for the body or the lower part will be too thin.

Figure 32. Making the straw angel.

6. Simple transparencies

General Instructions

When making transparencies it is best to start with a white background. A glass table with a lamp under it or a box with a light inside is very useful when making transparencies.

When choosing the colours take into account the mixed colours that will appear when two layers of differently coloured tissue-paper are laid one over the other. Sometimes the result is quite surprising!

Draw the outlines on the tissue-paper with a sharp pencil, because when you are cutting out the forms the pencil lines must be cut away too.

When cutting out the forms use a pair of small sharp scissors and take plenty of time because it is not as easy as it looks.

When gluing layers together use as little glue as possible and spread it as thinly as possible; blobs remain visible. Water-based glue is quite adequate and can be undone if necessary. However, a disadvantage of this kind of adhesive is that the sheets become unstuck after a time. A glue-stick can also be used.

Transparencies which are hung on the window can be subject to condensation even with double glazing. It is a good idea, therefore, to put a plastic sheet or saran wrap between the window and the transparency.

A simple window transparency

Materials
Tissue-papers of various colours
Tracing paper
Glue or glue-stick
A sharp pair of scissors

Method
The technique described here uses only tissue-paper which allows the colours full scope and provides endless variations.

The angel in Figure 33 is made from two

Figure 33. A simple angel transparency.

layers of yellow tissue-paper and a layer of white tissue-paper as cover.

First draw the design on the white tracing paper. Then for each layer of tissue-paper draw the requisite detailed copy on a separate sheet of tracing paper. The yellow angel thus consists of the two top figures in Figure 35.

Lay the first sheet of yellow tissue-paper on top of the first drawing and with a sharp pencil trace the figure. Cut it out. Lay the cut-out sheet on the second drawing and move it around until the two drawings fit. Then lay the second sheet of yellow tissue-paper exactly over the first, put the second drawing over and cut it out. Stick the two sheets together only at the edges at a few points, and do the same with the white sheet of tissue-paper. Finally, with a tiny bit of glue stick down any loose ends of the angel.

Figure 34. A development of Figure 33.

Figure 35. The different layers of tissue-paper.

33

Variation

The blue angel of Figure 34 has one layer more than the yellow angel: this transparency consists of two layers of light blue and one layer of pink or mauve tissue-paper. The instructions are the same.

When sticking them together make sure that the cut-out figures fit exactly over each other, the outside edge can be trimmed later.

Simple "stained glass" transparencies

Materials
Thick blue drawing-paper (160 gsm, 42 lb bond)
Tissue-paper in various colours
Tracing paper
Glue or a glue-stick
A pair of sharp scissors

Method
This technique gives the effect of stained glass panes set in lead.

First draw the design and the frame of the transparency on white tracing paper and then transfer the forms to the dark blue drawing-paper by using carbon paper; or you can draw the design straight on to the blue drawing-paper.

Cut out the design and the framework using sharp scissors or a knife (Figure 36).

Lay tissue-paper of the chosen colour on top of the drawing on the white tracing paper. The outlines of the drawing will be visible through the tissue-paper. With a pencil trace the figures

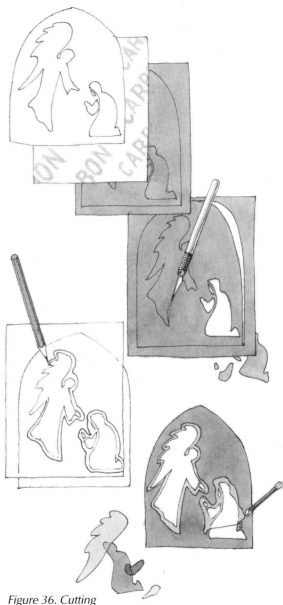

Figure 36. Cutting out the "stained glass" transparency.

34

Figure 37.

Figure 38.
▽

Figure 39.△

or details appropriate to this colour on to the tissue-paper. Try to ensure that the outlines on the tissue-paper are a fraction bigger than the original outlines on the drawing. Then cut out the figure on the coloured tissue-paper and stick this on at the back of the blue drawing-paper all round the opening. Use as little glue as possible. A good method is to use a matchstick to smear a tiny bit of glue along the edges of the drawing.

In this way stick colour by colour behind the opening. When two colours of tissue-paper are stuck over each other new colours are created.

Finally stick the transparency on to the window with two tiny strips of double-sided adhesive tape.

Variation 1: "Stained glass" window triptych
Make a simple triptych in the same way (Figure 38). The three colours of the shepherds are made here with two colours of tissue-paper. The shepherd on the left is made with brown tissue-paper except for his boots, and his

35

trousers and arms are also covered with red. The shepherd on the right requires green for his cap and purple for his shoes. Instead of one layer of a particular colour you can, of course, use two, as with Joseph's clothes and his staff.

Once the transparency is finished bend in the side pieces and put a night-light behind.

Variation 2: Window triptych
Instead of the stained glass window effect you can cut out a big "window" in the frame which takes out the greatest portion of the front of the triptych. First stick white tracing paper against the back of the opening. Cut out or tear out Christmas motifs from the tissue-paper and stick these on the back against the tracing paper.

Draw in the desired design first with a pencil on the tissue-paper before cutting it out. Tearing instead of cutting can give a very free effect. Using different layers of tissue-paper will give splendid colour shadings and depth.

7. Straw stars

Materials
Straws of natural colour
A sharp knife
Pointed scissors
A basin of water
An iron

Method
Soak the straws in water for about an hour. Cut down into the tops a little way with a sharp knife and iron them open further with a hot iron. You can also leave the wet straws uncut and iron them flat straight away.

Both the cut-open and the ironed straws can be made into very wide or into very narrow strips (cut with a ruler and a sharp knife). Straw stars made of cut-open straws have the disadvantage that they have a good side and a less good side, so that they look best against a background.

Straw stars made from straws which have not been cut open are the same on both sides, and so are more suitable for mobiles, for use on the Christmas tree or to be hung in front of a window.

In the examples given in this book gold thread is always used for suspending the stars; but any other colour can be used, for instance, red.

Cut the straws into two or three lengths depending on the size of the star.

Figure 40. Eight and sixteen-pointed stars. ▷

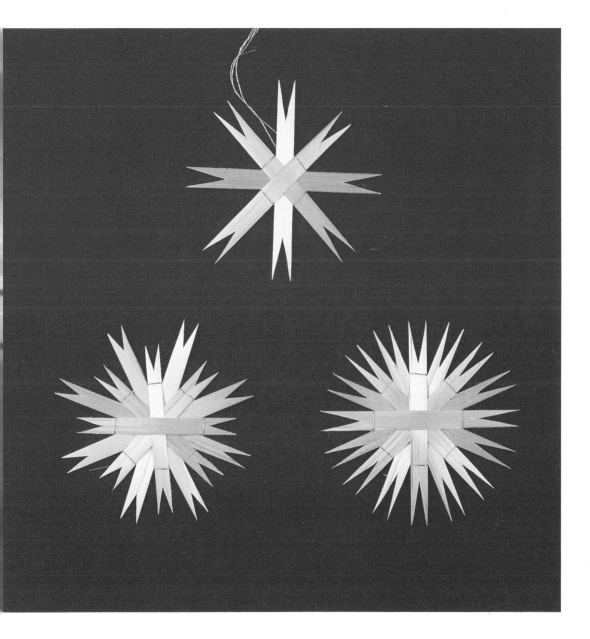

Eight-pointed star

Lay four straws of equal length crosswise upon each other. Put your forefinger on the point where the straws cross each other to hold them in place and weave a thread round the straws taking it first over the topmost straw, then under the next, then over the one after that, and so on (Figure 41). Finally tie the two ends of the thread together behind the star.

Alternatively, you could lay the straws crosswise on a block of wood and pin them down so that both hands are free to bind the straws together.

Cut the points of the stars to a particular shape (for examples, see Figure 42).

Sixteen-pointed star

Make two eight-pointed stars (as above) and lay one on top of the other. Bind the stars together with a thread in the same way as described above. The thread of one of the eight pointed stars can be cut away. In Figure 40 you can clearly see the binding thread of the eight-pointed star, and the second outside thread of the sixteen-pointed star.

With more practice you can make this star by laying all the straws for a sixteen-pointed star on top of each other at the same time, working the thread through them all and tying it up. Altering the length and width of the straws will vary the result. Stars with a greater number of points can be made. By alternating wide and narrow, short and long, flat and hollow straws you can make innumerable varieties (Figure 43).

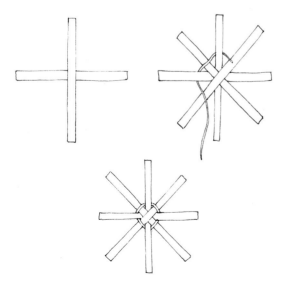

Figure 42. Cuts in the points of the star.

Figure 43. Stars with twelve, sixteen, twenty-four and ▷ thirty-two points.

Figure 41. Threading an eight-pointed star.

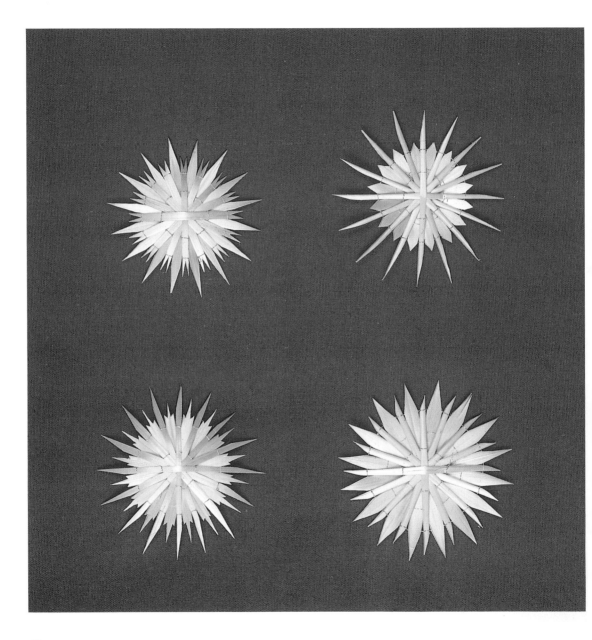

Large sixteen-pointed star with eight little stars round it

Select the widest straws for the sixteen-pointed star which consists of four short and four long flat straws (Figure 44). Take three narrower straws for each of the eight little surrounding stars; the fourth straw being already formed by the long straw of the sixteen-pointed star.

This combined star can of course be extended even further.

◁Figure 44. Variations of a sixteen-pointed star.

Figure 45. Large sixteen-pointed star with eight little stars.

Twelve-pointed star

Cut two flat straws into three pieces each. Lay the six pieces on top of each other as in the drawing, making first a simple saltire cross and then a double saltire cross (Figure 46). Lay the last straw horizontally; the first and last straw make a cross which encloses the other straws.

The thread with which the star is woven together comes from behind and goes over the last laid straw, under the next straw and so on (Figure 43, top left).

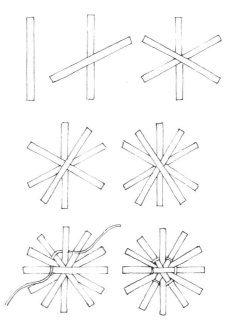

Figure 46. Threading a twelve-pointed star.

Stars with twenty-four and thirty-two points

For the star with twenty-four points lay one twelve-pointed star on another (see page 41), weave a thread through them and tie them together. If necessary cut off the surplus thread.

Variation
Use three wide and nine long narrow straws. First lay the three wide straws on top of each other (Figure 48) and then the three narrow straws behind them. Finally lay two straws against the star in front in the gaps between the narrow and the wide straws (Figure 47).

A star with thirty-two points is made in the same way as the star with twenty-four points, except that two stars with sixteen points are used. A similar star can also be made from four eight-pointed stars.

Figure 47. Star with twenty-four points.

Figure 48. Construction of a star with twenty-four points.

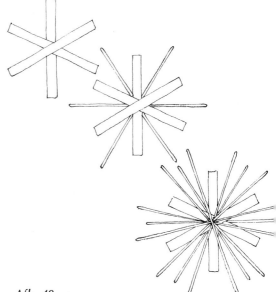

Afb. 48

Straw star mobile

This mobile has a large star of David with twelve twelve-pointed stars.

For the star of David take six wet whole straws. Lay three straws on top of each other to make an equilateral triangle and tie the ends together. With the other three straws make a similar triangle. Lay one triangle on top of the other to make the six-pointed star of David (Figure 49). Tie the stars together where they cross and suspend the mobile from four points (Figure 50).

Make the twelve-pointed stars from whole straws ironed flat: since these are heavier they hang well.

Suggestion for use: make this mobile during the time between Christmas and Three Kings' Day. Begin with the large star of David and each day add a twelve-pointed star.

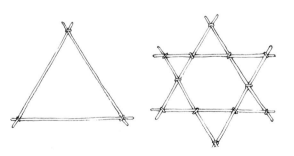

Figure 49. The star of David from which the other stars hang.

Figure 50. Straw star mobile. ▷

43

Great star with sixty-four points

This straw star which is shown in Figure 51 is made with 32 whole (unironed) straws. In this case the straws are worked while still *wet,* as they are more pliable and break less easily.

Make a star of eight straws by laying them crosswise on top of each other and tying them up. Make a second star in the same way.

Lay one star on top of the other, so that the rays interlock. Tie the star together with a fresh thread. The result is a star with thirty-two points.

Make a second star with thirty-two points, lay one star on top of the other and tie them together with a fresh thread, to make the star with sixty-four points.

The straws must still be wet when you finish the ends.

Figure 51. Star with sixty-four points.

8. Folded transparent stars

General instructions

Materials
Kite-paper (transparency paper) or tissue-paper
Transparent glue or a glue-stick
Double-sided adhesive tape
A sharp knife

Transparent stars are made by folding each piece of transparent paper into a single star-point and then assembling these single star-points to make a star.

To make transparent stars use kite-paper or tissue-paper (see "Materials," page 84).

Kite-paper (transparency paper) is sufficiently transparent and is more robust than tissue-paper, so it is more easily worked.

Tissue-paper is less colour-fast than kite-paper and since transparent stars are usually left to hang for a long time, tissue-paper stars can quickly lose their colour in the increasing strength of the sunlight.

When choosing the colours remember that the pattern in the transparent stars emerges from the different layers of paper laid upon each other. Thus dark colours are not suitable for complicated stars. Yellow, orange, pale green and rose are best.

Do not make transparent stars too small because it is more difficult to make the folds exact.

The models shown in this book have a diameter of 8" (20 cm).

The sizes of the pieces are important, because if the sizes are altered, the pattern changes too. An example of this is shown in Figures 62 and 63, where the width of the pieces to be folded are respectively 3" and 1¾" (7.5 and 4.5 cm).

Before making the star-points you can experiment with:

oblong sheets (for instance 4" × 3", 10 × 7.5 cm). Here it is the length of the sheet which determines the dimensions of the star. In our example then twice 4" is 8" (10 cm, 20 cm).

square sheets (e. g. 3" × 3", 7.5 × 7.5 cm); in this case it is the diagonal which determines the dimensions of the star. A sheet 3" × 3" has a diagonal of a little over 4" (10 cm). The diagonal is a little over one third longer than the sides of the square.

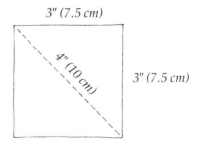

Work out beforehand how many pieces can be obtained from one large sheet, this avoids wastage. You can get a hundred 4" × 3" (10 × 7.5 cm) oblong sheets out of a 30" × 40" (75 × 102 cm) sheet of kite-paper or from the same sheet a hundred and thirty 3" × 3" (7.5 × 7.5 cm) sheets.

45

Make sure that the pieces are exactly the same size; to achieve this, first fold the large sheet exactly in two (with a sharp crease) and slit in two with a sharp knife. Then fold these two sheets in two and cut them. Continue in this way until you have obtained the desired size. A guillotine or trimmer is very useful for this. In order to obtain a different shape of sheet, narrower, wider or longer it is advisable first to cut a strip off the large sheet, so that exact measurements are obtained.

It is important to fold the sheets as exactly as possible because any divergence shows up clearly in the final result.

The creases must be really sharp. When the same points have to be folded twice as in Figure 61b then do not make the first fold come exactly to the centre line but allow a tiny space (about 1 mm) in between. Ensure that the sides come exactly together with the second fold.

It is advisable to stick down all the folded parts using transparent glue, adhesive or a glue-stick. Non-transparent adhesive becomes visible immediately the star is hung up. Make sure that you do not use too much glue on the paper.

Finally stick the stars to the window with strips of double-sided adhesive tape. Use only very small strips and stick them to the parts where the star is least transparent (the points) then the tape will not be seen. If the strips of adhesive tape are too large it is difficult to prevent the star from becoming damaged when it is taken down again.

Stars from square pieces

Simple eight-pointed star

Materials
8 square pieces of kite-paper (transparency paper), for example 3" × 3" (7.5 × 7.5 cm)

Method
With stars made from square pieces the diagonal is the central fold. Work according to the following steps:
1. Fold the sheets across the diagonal so that points B and C meet. Unfold again (Figure 53a).

Figure 52. Simple eight-pointed star.

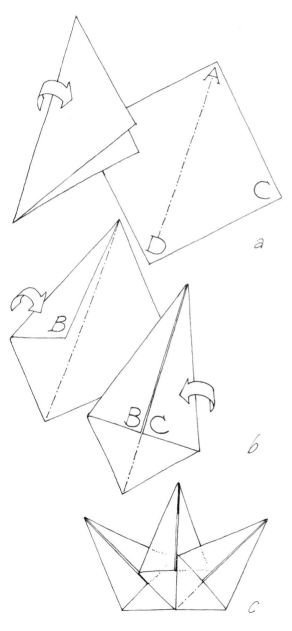

2. Fold points B and C in to the diagonal (Figure 53b); stick them down with a spot of glue.
3. When all eight sheets are folded in this way stick the star carefully together, sticking the unfolded bottom of the first star-point to the diagonal of the next (Figure 53c) continuing until all the points have been stuck together. The result is shown on Figure 52.

Variation 1: Ten-pointed star
In a ten-pointed star the corners must overlap each other more than is shown on Figure 53c. Figure 54 illustrates the effect of rays at the heart of the star which results.

◁ *Figure 53. Folding an eight-pointed star.*

Figure 54. Ten-pointed star.

Variation 2: Eight-pointed star

The eight-pointed star described above was very simple to fold. With a slight variation the whole pattern of the star can be altered.

After the second step open the flaps and fold points B and C to the newly made crease and close the flaps again. Stick down securely (Figure 56). Then stick the star together as in step 3 above. For the result see Figure 55.

Variations 3 and 4: Five and ten-pointed star

By taking five instead of eight folded points you can make an interesting modification in the pattern of the star of Figure 55. In Figure 57 you can see that the overlap of each individual point of the star is no longer a half point as shown on Figure 53c, but only a fraction of it (in our

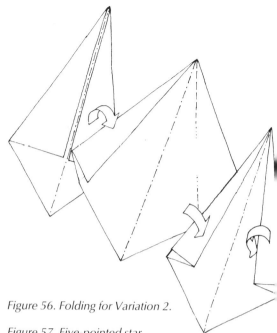

Figure 56. Folding for Variation 2.

Figure 55. Eight-pointed star.

Figure 57. Five-pointed star.

48

example where the star is approximately 8", 20 cm across, the overlap is ³/₈"–¹/₂", 10–12 mm). In this way a five-pointed star motif appears in the middle.

By doubling the number of points a splendid ten-pointed star appears (Figure 58).

There are two ways of going from a five-pointed star to a ten-pointed star (or from a four-pointed star to an eight-pointed star and on to a sixteen-pointed star).

The simplest way is to make two five-pointed stars and stick one on top of the other. The more exact method is to first assemble a five-pointed star and then stick the remaining five points one by one between the points of the star already made.

Variation 5: eleven-pointed star

A new pattern appears when after the first two steps of the folding pattern the points are folded further.

Fold the lower half (that is, the part which will be the centre of the star) of the two sides once (Figure 59), and stick the fold down towards the centre line, then, as in Variation 2 for the upper half, open the flaps and fold the points B and C to the newly-made crease and close the flaps again.

Fold eleven loose points instead of ten and stick these together to produce the star of Figure 60. In this Figure it can clearly be seen how far over each other the separate points must be stuck.

Figure 58. Ten-pointed star.

Figure 59. Folding for Variation 5.

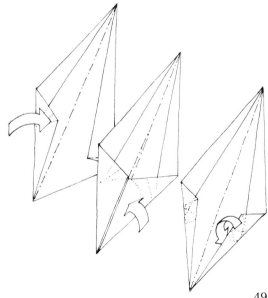

49

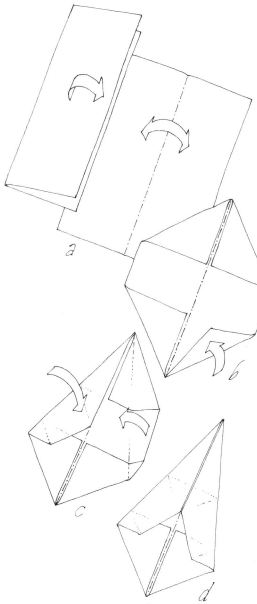

Figure 60. An eleven-pointed star.

Stars from oblong sheets

Simple eight-pointed star

With stars from oblong sheets the centre line is the central fold. Work as follows:

1. Fold the sheets lengthwise and unfold them again (Figure 61a)
2. Fold the four corners in to the centre line so that a point is made above and below (Figure 61b). We recommend that the corners be stuck down with a bit of glue.
3. From the top point fold the two sides once again to the centre line (Figure 61c). This sharp point makes one of the points of the

◁ *Figure 61. Folding for an eight-pointed star.*
Figure 62. An eight-pointed star.

star; the wider lower points form the middle of the star.

4. Once all the eight points have been folded stick the star carefully together as shown in step 3 on page 47 (Figure 53c).

Variation 1
For the eight-pointed star in Figure 62, 4″ × 3″ (10 × 7.5 cm) sheets are used. By using the same formula with narrower sheets, for example 4″ × 1¾″ (10 × 4.5 cm) the star in Figure 63 appears.

Variation 2
Make a centre line as in step 1, but fold in only the two top corners to the centre line. Unfold them again, halve them and tuck the edge

Figure 64. Folding for Variation 2. ▷

Figure 63. An eight-pointed star, Variation 1.

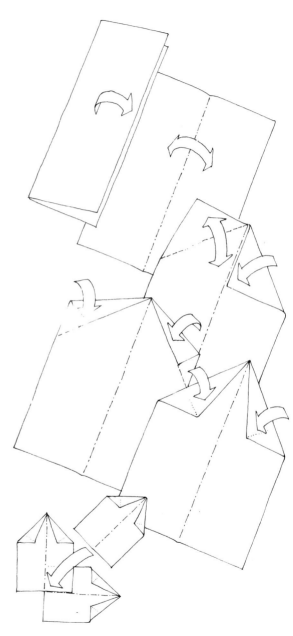

inside as you fold it again (Figure 64). Stick down. The unfolded parts form the centre of the star, so the star is assembled by first using four pieces to make a star with four corners, after which the remaining points are inserted between the first four (Figures 64 and 65).

Variation 3

Fold the sheets as directed in steps 1 and 2 (Figure 61). Unfold the two sides of the bottom point which will form the centre of the star. Fold the two points to the crease and then inwards, so that a new form appears (Figure 66a and b).

Finish off with steps 3 and 4 of page 51 (also shown in Figure 66c and d). The result is shown on Figure 67.

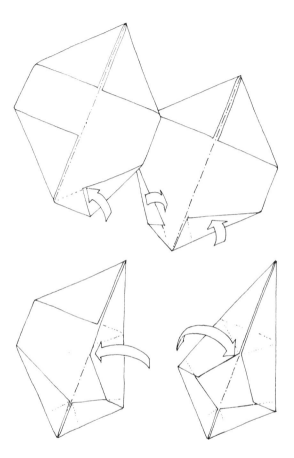

Figure 66. Folding for Variation 3. ▷

Figure 65. An eight-pointed star, Variation 2.

Variation 4

Follow steps 1 and 2. Unfold the lower flaps (the ones that come to the centre of the star) so that the square reappears. By folding carefully diagonally, you can find the midpoint of the fold-line (Figure 69a). Then fold the outer point to the midpoint of the fold-line and refold both sides along the fold-line to the middle. Finish off with steps 3 and 4 (Figure 69c and d). The result can be seen in Figure 68.

Figure 67. Variation 3. △ ▽*Figure 68. Variation 4.*

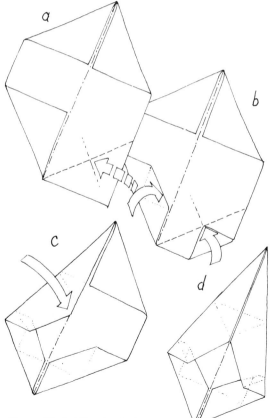

Figure 69. Folding for Variation 4.

A sixteen-pointed star

Fold the sixteen points of this star according to steps 1–3 of Figure 61.

To stick them together proceed as follows: first stick two points together as shown in Figure 53c (page 47) and then stick the third point between the first two. Then stick the fourth point on to the third, the fifth on to the second, and so on.

Because with this star many layers of paper are folded and stuck on top of each other it is important to use a lightly coloured transparent paper.

A sharply pointed eight-pointed star

Figure 70. A sixteen-pointed star. ▲

For an eight-pointed star with sharper points follow the first steps as for the simple eight-pointed star on page 51. The character of the star is greatly altered because the sheets are narrower. The star of Figure 71 uses half the original measurements for the sheets: that is, 4″ × 1½″ (10 × 3.7 cm). After steps 1, 2 and 3 of pages 51 and 52 there is a last fold as in Figure 72a in which the sides of the top point are folded again to the middle. For a star with sharp points we recommend that you take a bigger scale with very narrow sheets, otherwise the work becomes very fiddly.

Figure 71. A sharply pointed star. ▷

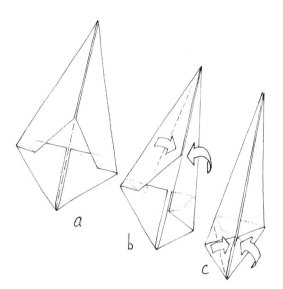

a

b

c

Variations 1 and 2: sharp-pointed sixteen-pointed stars

For the stars in Figures 73 and 74 the same applies as for the sixteen-pointed star. Here we can see the resemblance with the broad sixteen-pointed star of Figure 70, although the ray motif emerges more clearly with the sharp points.

The star of Figure 73 is folded in the same way as the sharp-pointed eight-pointed star.

For the star in Figure 74 make the extra fold as in Figure 72b. Proceed with step 3 and stick the star together as described for the sixteen-pointed star on page 55.

Figure 72. Folding for a sharply pointed star.

Figure 73. Variation 1.

Figure 74. Variation 2.

56

An eight-pointed star from square pieces

For this star (Figure 75) take eight square pieces, say 4" × 4" (10 cm × 10 cm). Proceed as follows:

1. First fold the pieces in half and unfold again.
2. Fold the corners of the square to the inside (Figure 76) to make the square ABCD; unfold the points again.
3. Halve the triangles now formed and fold them in again to make the square ABCD again. In the middle a diamond is left free.
4. Finally fold points A and C to the centre line; the star points are now finished.
5. Stick this eight-pointed star together as described in Figure 53c (page 47).

Figure 75. An eight-pointed star.

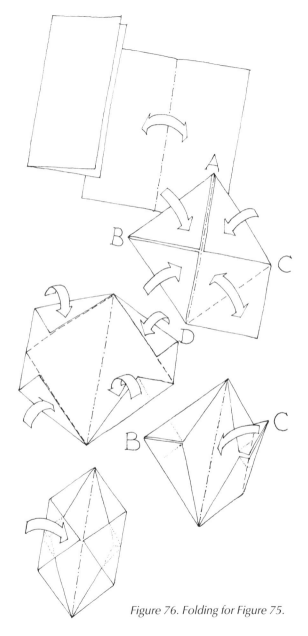

Figure 76. Folding for Figure 75.

9. Christmas stables

A clay stable

A stable can be made with clay as simply (Figure 77) as you wish. Children can make these stables by themselves.

What matters most with these simple stables is the landscape in which they are placed: the surroundings must create an atmosphere. Indicate such a landscape with a dark brown or green cloth and lay some stones, moss or pine-cones on it. Make trees by sticking a sprig of green in a lump of clay.

Figure 77. A simple clay stable.

One suggestion is to let the children make something for each Sunday during Advent. For the first Sunday they can make the stable, for the second Sunday they can make some bushes and trees to go round it, for the third Sunday some sheep, for the fourth Sunday the people, Joseph, Mary and the shepherds, and for Christmas the angel and the Child.

Make the figures in one piece. Do not make arms, legs and head and then stick them on to the body because once the clay dries the separate parts are liable to fall off. Once the stable is dry it can be coloured with water-colours if desired.

Stable with shepherds

Materials
White and brown unspun sheep's wool
Pink knitted cotton
Coloured scraps of cloth and felt
Scraps of fur
Unspun Shetland wool or camel-hair

Method
For each figure work a tuft of teased white wool into a firm roll approximately 3½" (9 cm) long.

Wrap a piece of doll's knitted cotton round it and tie it off to make the head.

Make a fairly close-fitting garment from a thicker woollen material or felt to cover the rest of the roll of wool, so that the figure can stand (Figure 78). Gather the cloth in at the neck.

Mary has a robe of red felt, with a cloak made of a square piece of blue cloth or felt. Drape the cloak round her head and fasten with a few stitches at the head and the neck. The hands are made of some teased sheep's wool covered with knitted cotton. Sew them on between the folds of the cloak.

Draw in the eyes and mouth with a fine pencil.

Joseph and the shepherds have capes of cloth or fur. Secure these at the neck and at the centre front with a few stitches. A stick can then be inserted between the cape and the body. The hair is made of teased brown sheep's wool secured with the hat.

The hat consists of a round piece of felt. You can form the hat by gathering it. Sew the hat on to the head with a few stitches (Figure 78).

The Child is made in the same way as the other dolls, only a little smaller. When the head is finished wrap the rest of the body in a cloth of light-coloured material, flannel or felt. Secure the cloth with a few stitches.

Make the **sheep** from a rectangular piece of fur or fleece. Roll this in from the narrow end. Sew up at the bottom and if necessary at the ends using a leatherwork needle. Tie off about one third to make the head. Now clip the sheep to give it a good shape. Make ears of soft leather or felt and sew them on (Figure 79).

Figure 78.

Ox and ass. Turn in the ends of a little skein. of carded unspun Shetland wool; from this form a lying ass with a few loose stitches and a fine thread. Make the ears by gently pulling out the wool.

For the ox, camel-hair or light brown, teased sheep's wool is very suitable.

The stable can be built of pieces of bark and twigs nailed or stuck together; use single large pieces of bark for the roof. The stable can then be furnished with straw, moss, plants, stones, and so on.

A more detailed sheep

Materials
4 pipe-cleaners
White unspun wool
A darning-needle
Crochet hook No. 3
An old pair of scissors or pliers
Glue

Method
For the head of the sheep bend the end of a pipe-cleaner round two fingers and twist it round the neck (Figure 81). Make a kink for the neck.

For the forelegs bend a pipe-cleaner round the body; and do the same for the hindlegs. Cut the feet to shape only when the sheep is completely finished. Use the fourth pipe-cleaner to give the frame more stability and to lengthen the tail. Bend the end of the first

Figure 79. Making sheep.

60

pipe-cleaner to the front and twist it round the body.

Tease a bit of wool out and begin working it round the sheep at the stomach. After each turn let go the tuft to avoid getting it twisted. Continue working round the sheep evenly from the body to the head and back again to the hind parts until it is thick enough. Keep winding the wool to the last fibre, this will prevent it from unravelling. Do not work to the very end of the nose, or the wool will slip off.

Work the shoulders and the hindlegs as follows: hold one end of the piece of wool

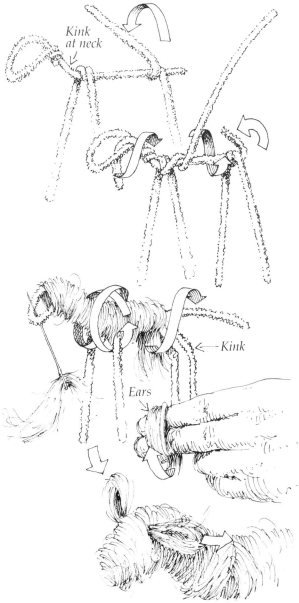

Figure 81. Making the more detailed sheep. ▷

Figure 80. A more detailed sheep.

tightly on to the left shoulder, take the wool. down behind the left foreleg and back up obliquely over the chest, over the neck, crosswise over the breast to the right foreleg, back behind it and so on. In this way you form a figure of eight. Do not work the wool too tightly and make sure that it lies flat on the back. Work the hindquarters in the same way. Do not make the head too thick.

The nose. Thread a bit of wool through the darning-needle and secure the nose. Cover the front part also with wool (Figure 81).

The tail. Push the wool towards the hindquarters so that the pipe-cleaner of the tail stands free. Wind a tuft of wool over half of the pipe-cleaner. Bend the pipe-cleaner back half way, so that the end of the tail is covered with wool. the tail should now be 1" (2.5 cm) long. Finish off the bent-back tail with another tuft of wool, giving the tail a nice shape.

The legs. Push the wool of the body up a bit and wind good thin tufts of wool round the legs about halfway down. Put some glue on the lower half of the legs and continue to wind on wool. Allow the glue to dry properly and finish off by cutting the legs to the right size.

The ears. Wind a bit of wool regularly round two fingers and remove. Thrust the crochet hook carefully through the right place through the head. Catch the wool in the hook and pressing your fingers on the other side of the head pull the hook through. Take both ears between your thumb and forefinger and rub them into shape. Let the ears hang and fasten them with needle and thread.

Ox and ass can be made in the same way.

10. Transparencies with partitions

Materials
Gold cardstock or cardboard
Thick and thin (white) cardstock
Various coloured tissue-papers
Tracing paper
A pair of scissors or a knife
Glue
2 sheets of blue paper (letter or A4, not too thin)

Method
A transparency built with several partitions, with spaces between, one behind the other, gives a wonderful perspective and a deeper dimension to the whole. You can place a light behind the partitions or, remarkably, in front.

Figures 82, 84 and 86 show three different transparencies with partitions. The first two are made in the same way.

The transparency in Figure 82 consists of a golden frame in front of the first partition, a narrow mid-partition which simply indicates the ground and the back partition.

The transparency in Figure 84 has three mid-partitions, the first simply indicates the ground.

The stable in Figure 86 relies on the same principle, but the mid-partitions are fixed in a rather different way.

The number of partitions is partly determined by the intended design. The fact that on the left hand side of the transparency in Figure 84 two shepherds and Mary have been placed one behind the other means that already three mid-partitions are necessary. Bear this in mind when you are making a transparency. It is technically possible to make more partitions, but it does not necessarily make the transparency more beautiful.

By following the description of the transparency of Figure 84 you will understand the principle and will be able to make other transparencies.

Figure 82. A partition transparency.

Begin by sketching the total picture with all the objects and figures which will have a place in the partitions. Do this in the same size as the transparency is to be made. A good size is 8" (20 cm) high and 10" (25 cm) wide.

Decide how many partitions will be necessary for your sketch. To make the operation easier give each partition a number, beginning at the front. The transparency of Figure 84 has 5 partitions. If you are inexperienced in making partition-transparencies it is best first to draw each separate partition with all the figures belonging to it, to make sure they fit.

Determine the outer shape of the transparency and so of all the partitions. Cut the frame for the first partition (the front) from gold card. Make this one slightly larger than the others, so that the latter recede into the background behind it. Cut the other partitions from thick white cardstock (each slightly smaller than the one in front). Cut out the inside of each partition making sure the "ground" becomes progressively higher as we go back; this increases the perspective. These partitions do not have any trees or figures.

Cut out the people and the animals from the thinner white cardstock, and in this case also the crib. Make the figures rather narrow, the art is to dress them with bits of tissue-paper at the front. Fold the clothes and stick them on loosely making sure that the clothes project beyond the figures. The tissue-paper being loosely stuck on and billowing (see, for example, Joseph and Mary in Figure 82) makes the picture of the transparency come alive.

When dressing, begin with the face and the hands, only subsequently stick on the clothing. The foremost shepherd's crook is stuck to his hands only after he has been dressed. Also the

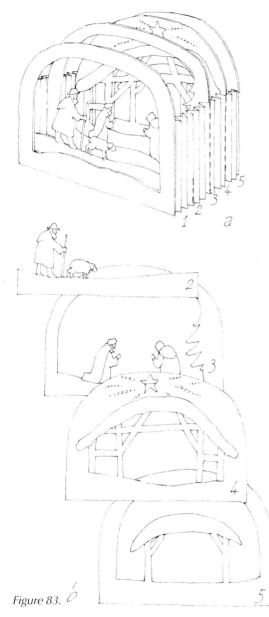

Figure 83.

child is cut out separately before being placed in the crib. (Figure 85a).

With the ox and the ass draw only the visible parts. Make the animals rather larger so that they can be stuck straight away into the stable. The lamb in the foreground is stuck with little wads of white tissue-paper.

The people and the animals are now dressed, but the partitions are still bare.

Partition No. 2 has moss and grass; when you are sticking it together remember that the tissue-paper must protrude at the top.

This applies also to the second mid-partition (No. 3). In this one we can possibly stick another tree with green tissue-paper at the sides.

The third mid-partition (No. 4) is more difficult. Begin by sticking blue tissue-paper round the stable to make the sky. Only when the glue is dry cut out the star and its rays from the blue tissue-paper using a sharp knife. Stick yellow tissue-paper at the back of the partition to form the starry sky. Make the timbers of the stable with dark yellow tissue-paper which should also stick out.

Cover the last partition (No. 5) wholly with white tracing paper. Now cover the front of this partition with light yellow tissue-paper. Make the yellow a bit darker and bring some design into it by sticking several layers of tissue-paper over each other at the back of the partition in such a way that the transparency becomes progressively darker towards the edges.

It is better not to stick the space above the stable so that the candle-light can shine better on to the star in partition No. 4. Now stick the figures into their places. The crib comes into the

Figure 84. A partition transparency.

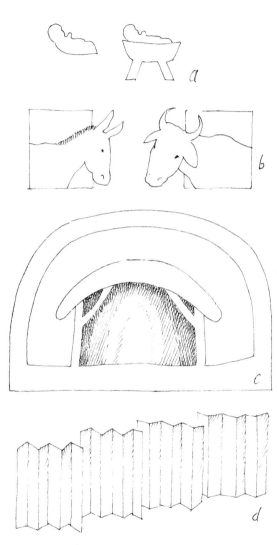

middle of the fourth partition with Mary and Joseph on each side, while the animals look on from the sides between the timbers.

From the blue paper cut two pieces and fold them together like a concertina (Figure 85d). Stick the partitions together at both sides with the folded strips, making sure that between two partitions there is always at least one zigzag.

In the transparency described here, we have allowed more space between the second and the third partition, because this shepherd is still in the fields and not in the stable. The depth of the transparency should now be 3"–4" (8–10 cm). This prevents it from falling over. In the simple partition-transparency of Figure 82, the gap between the three partitions is made rather bigger to give the transparency stability.

◁ *Figure 85. Making the partition transparency.*

Figure 86. A partition transparency.

Figure 86 shows a stable with a roof. This transparency is basically made in the same way as described above, but the partitions are not joined together by concertinas, but with a hinge stuck to the side (Figure 87). With this transparency first stick all the partitions together before attaching the roof to the stable and fixing the doors to the sides. It is easier to stick the stable to the back when everything is finished. Furthermore in this case it is also possible to put single figures in front of the stable.

Whereas the partitions of the other two transparencies create an effect of spaciousness, in the stable we create an enclosed space by making the inside of the foremost partition rather smaller, done here with the timbers.

Figure 87. Transparency with a roof.

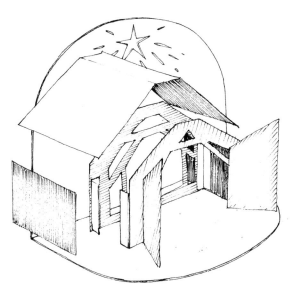

11. Pentagonal transparencies

Materials
Gold cardstock or cardboard
Tracing paper
Tissue-paper
Transparent glue and/or a glue-stick
A thread
A sharp knife or pair of scissors
Ruler and pencil

Method
Transparencies showing a five-pointed star (Figures 88–91, see also the title-page) are not difficult for children to make, and quickly give a good result. These transparencies can be hung up in front of the window.

Cut out a pentagon from the gold or different coloured card. There are different sizes of pentagons on page 81 as a pattern. Draw a second pentagon inside the first at a distance of ³/₄″ (2 cm) from the edge. Cut this second pentagon out of the card so that a frame of gold card is left. Do not make the frame any narrower in case the card starts to bend when the tissue-paper is stuck on to it.

First cover the back with white tracing paper. Place a triangle of tissue-paper over three corners of the pentagon joining two opposite points and completely covering the point between (Figure 89). Stick the edges of the tissue-paper along the two sides of the pentagon. Take another triangle and join the next two corners together. Continue in this way until all the corners are joined up. It is important that the long edge of each triangle is cut leanly and straight, as this edge is visible.

It is advisable to stick the tissue-paper together with a tiny bit of glue or glue-stick. Inside the frame you will now have a five-pointed star with another pentagon in the middle with the apex pointing downwards.

Finally stick a thread to the top of the frame to suspend the transparency. If you stick the transparency on to a window with double-sided adhesive tape there is the danger that when you want to take it down again you will tear the tissue-paper.

Figure 89. Making the pentagonal transparency. ▷

Figure 88. A pentagonal transparency.

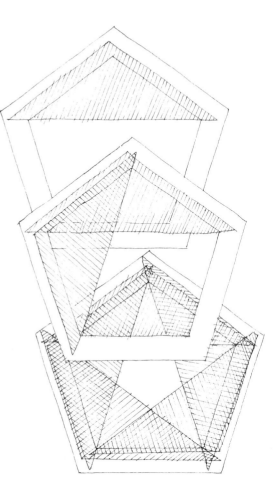

Variation 1

Make a transparency as described above. When the star inside the frame is finished repeat the procedure, reducing the size of the triangles of tissue-paper by $1/4''$ (5 mm). In this way a second five-pointed star appears. Repeat until you reach the edge of the frame. Remember from time to time to stick the pieces of tissue-paper together in the middle with a tiny bit of glue. Finish off the outside of the frame by cutting away all superfluous bits of tissue-paper (Figure 90).

The variation described above can also be carried out with various colours as shown in the illustration on the title-page. With this transparency the colour is deepened by working with several colours (white, yellow and orange) in contrast to that in Figure 90 where several layers of the same colour are laid one upon the other. In this way we can obtain endless variations. Choose a colour that is not too dark or the transparency will not admit light at the edges where there are several layers.

Variation 2

The frame can also be varied, as shown on Figure 91 where the outside is round.

The transparent star inside the frame appears to be very complicated but this variation can be obtained in a very simple manner. First make a five-pointed star as shown in Figure 88. Then take strips of tissue-paper about ³⁄₈″ (1 cm) wide and with these join the two opposite corners of the pentagon in such a way that half of the strip is stuck over the star already made while the other half falls inside. Where the strip has been stuck over the star already made, the darker bands will appear. Here, too, innumerable variations can be achieved. Be sure not to use too much glue, or it may cause colour differences in the tissue-paper.

Figure 90. A pentagonal transparency.

Figure 91. A pentagonal transparency.

12. Geometrical figures

Materials
Gold foil
A fine pair of scissors or a sharp knife
A pencil with a sharp point
Glue
A ruler

Tetrahedron made of gold foil

A tetrahedron is a regular solid figure contained by four regular (equilateral) triangles (Figure 92).

Figure 92. Tetrahedron and cube.

Copy the pattern of Figure 93, or alternatively follow the instructions on page 79 to construct the shapes in any size.

Lay the sheet of paper with the copied pattern on the back of the gold foil, and stick it on with two little bits of adhesive tape so that it will not slip. Then draw in the whole form on to the foil. Remove the paper and cut the form out of the foil. To get good sharp creases it is advisable to fold and unfold the crease a few times before sticking down.

Spread the glue thinly on both surfaces to be stuck. Wait until the glue is nearly dry and then stick the tetrahedron together, sticking a suspension thread to the inside before closing it. Tie a few knots at the bottom of the thread so that it will not slip out of the tetrahedron. Make sure that the corners join together as exactly as possible because the glued parts are not easy to unstick again.

Cube made of gold foil

A cube consists of six squares. A pattern for sticking a cube together is shown on Figure 94. This can be copied or traced. If you prefer to construct you own pattern, there are instructions on page 79. The procedure is the same as that of the tetrahedron. Before sticking down the lid stick a suspension thread to the inside of one of the corners.

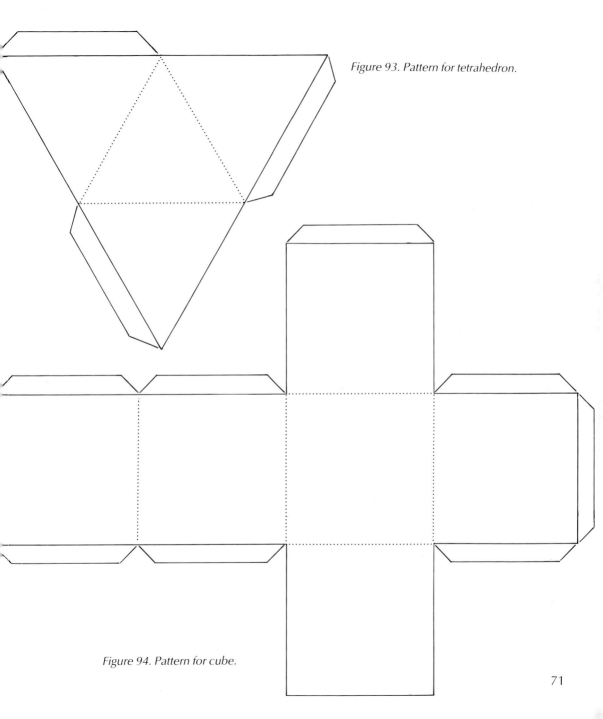

Figure 93. Pattern for tetrahedron.

Figure 94. Pattern for cube.

71

Icosahedron made of gold foil

The icosahedron consists of twenty equilateral triangles (Figure 95). In Figure 96 the pattern is shown unfolded. The construction of the icosahedron follows easily upon that of the tetrahedron. Remember to fold all the lines before beginning to glue the model, because afterwards this is no longer possible. It is important to leave one of the triangles open to the end, so that you can even out any irregularities from the inside using a pencil.

Figure 96. Pattern for an icosahedron. ▷

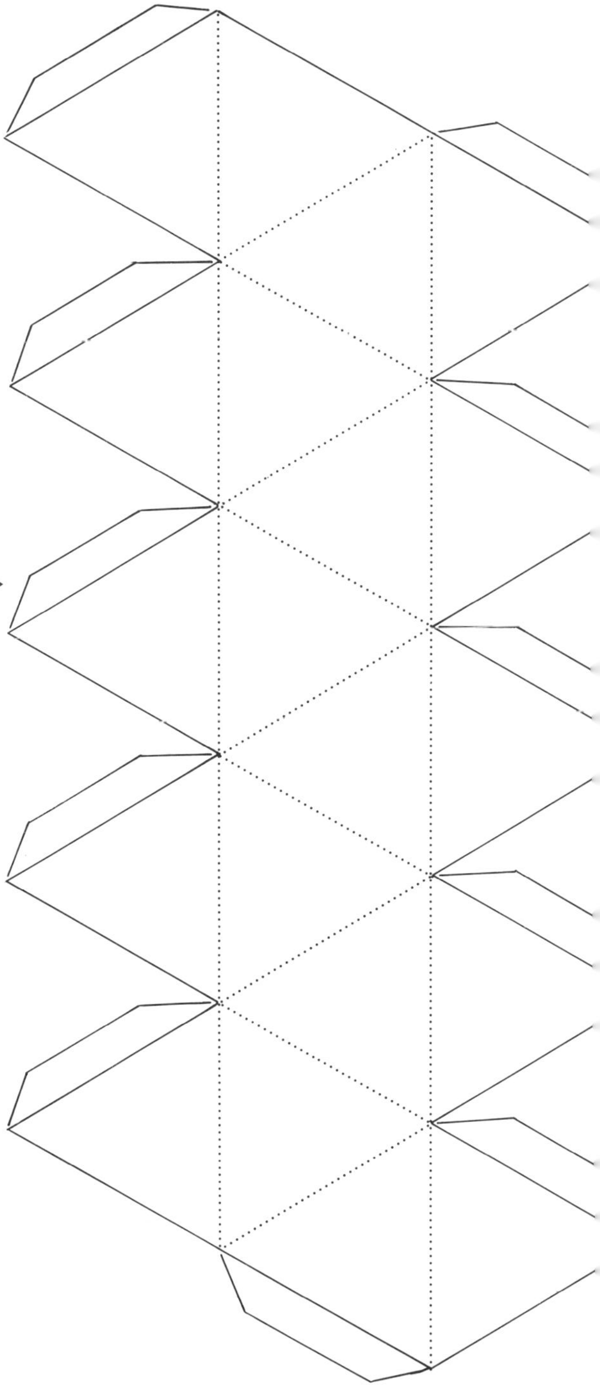

Figure 95. An icosahedron.

Dodecahedron made of gold foil

This figure consists of twelve regular pentagons (Figure 98). Figure 97 shows a pattern for six pentagons which make up half of the dodecahedron. When the six pentagons are stuck together they make a bowl. Two such bowls fit exactly together as can be seen in Figure 21 on page 24, but in this model only the lower bowl needs sticking edges (marked **x**), not both bowls. The best method is to stick the bottom-half together completely, and when sticking the top half together, leave the "lid" open. If

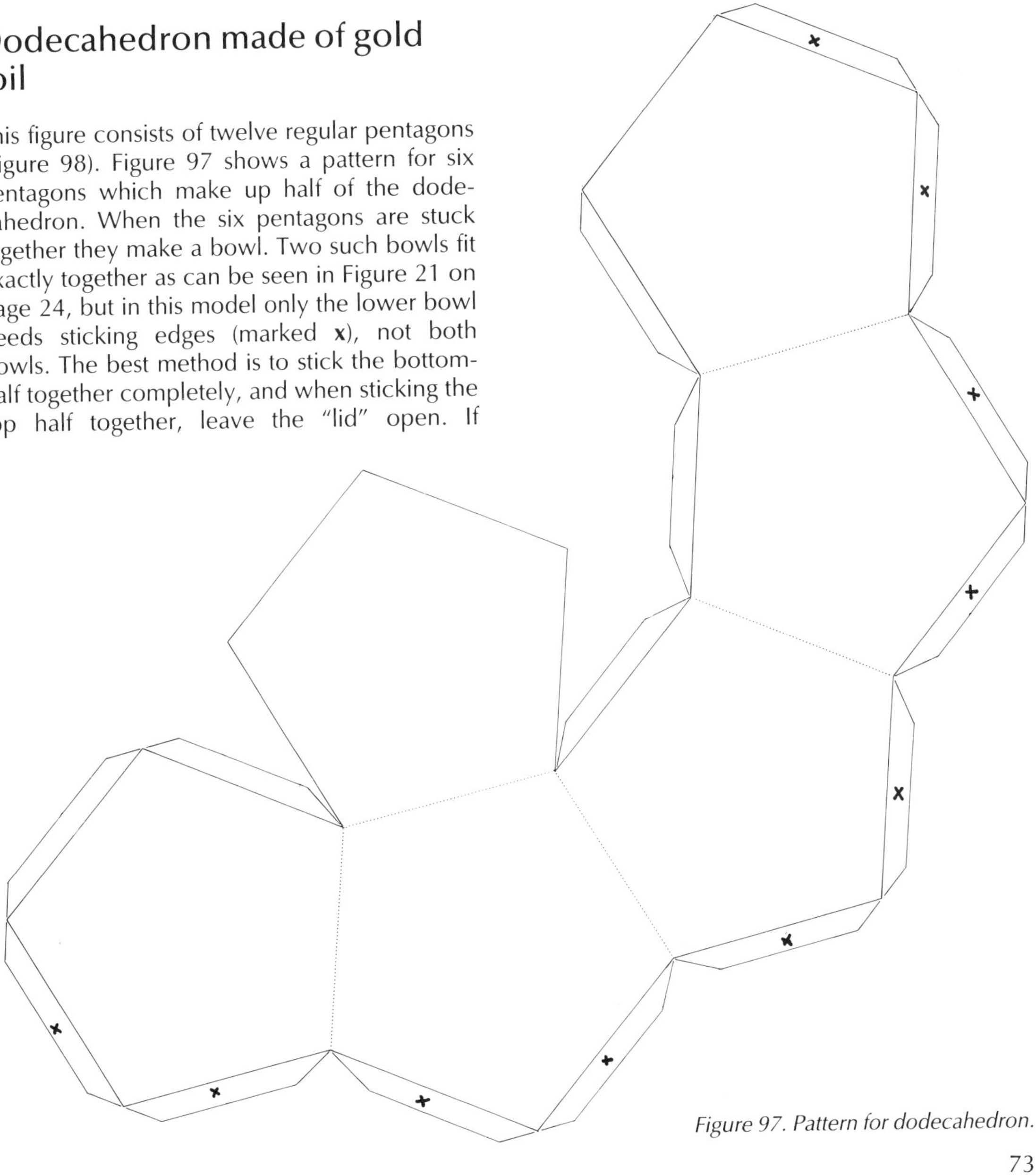

Figure 97. Pattern for dodecahedron.

necessary the sticking edges can be pressed with a pencil from the inside and any irregularities removed. Before sticking down the lid stick a thread to the inside of one of the corners.

Three-dimensional star made of gold foil

From a dodecahedron a three-dimensional star can be made (Figure 100). For this make twelve pentagonal pyramids, the base of each being the same size as that of the dodecahedron (Figure 99) and stick one pyramid on to each pentagon.

In the same way a three-dimensional star can be made from an icosahedron, in this case use twenty three-sided pyramids.

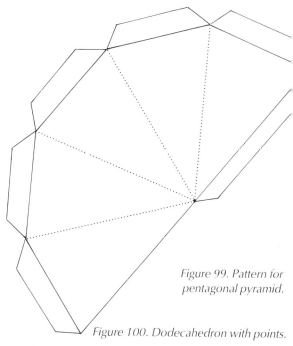

Figure 99. Pattern for pentagonal pyramid.

Figure 98. Dodecahedron.

Figure 100. Dodecahedron with points.

Dodecahedron made of straw

Materials
Straws
A ruler
A sharp knife
Elastic adhesive tape
Glue
Some strong paper
A pair of scissors
A little thread

Method
This dodecahedron consists of twelve regular five-pointed stars (Figure 101). As a guide to determining the size of this three-dimensional

Figure 101. Straw dodecahedron.

figure, note that if the sides of a five-pointed star are 2″ (5 cm), the diameter of the whole dodecahedron will be about 3¼″ (8 cm).

Use cut-open ironed straws (see "Straw stars" on page 36). Cut the straws into thin strips with the help of a sharp knife and a (steel) ruler.

For a dodecahedron sixty (12 × 5) straws are

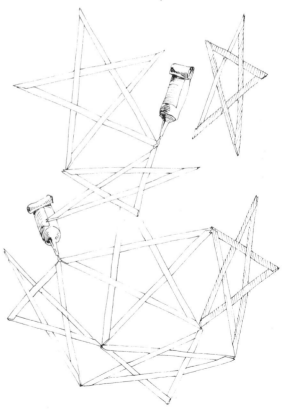

Figure 102. Making the pentagrams.

needed. Calculate therefore how many strips can be obtained from the length of one straw.

For this three-dimensional form it is very important that the five-pointed stars are as exact as possible and of the same size. A practical method of simultaneously making the straws all the same size is to mark off the length desired on a piece of thick drawing-paper. Lay all the straws on the paper between the marks. Stick the straws together with some elastic adhesive tape. Clip them to size with a pair of scissors along the marks.

Construct a five-pointed star of the same size as the star which you wish to make (for the construction see page 80). Use this as a template for sticking the star together.

Take five straws and lay them with the shiny side down; it is advisable always to select five straws of approximately the same width for each five pointed-star. Apply a little glue to the ends of two straws, one on the shiny side, one on the dull side (use a tube with a very fine nozzle, for example model-building glue). Allow the glue to dry a bit and then stick the end of the other straw on to it firmly. Figure 102 shows the five straws interwoven to make a five-pointed star with the third straw worked under one of the two other straws. Apply glue to one of the ends of the two straws stuck together, allow it to dry a bit and stick on the third straw. In the same way stick the last two straws. Lay the star on the pentagram on the paper to check whether the star is regular. If necessary adjust the points till the correct form has been obtained, but once the glue sets it is no longer possible to change the shape of the star.

Make all the stars in this way and allow them to set.

Now join the stars together to form a dode-cahedron by applying a little glue to all five points of the first three stars. Allow the glue to dry a bit. Stick two stars together at two points. Place one of these stars on a block of wood as a base and ease the other star up so that the third star can be joined to the pair (Figure 102).

Apply glue to the points of the next three stars and allow to dry. Stick these stars to the free points of the three stars already joined. Now half of the dodecahedron is finished.

Proceed in the same way until the whole star is finished. When you are sticking the last star on use a little more glue on one of the points so that you can attach a gold suspension thread.

Figure 103. Two straw dodecahedrons.

Variation 1

It is possible with the separated five-pointed stars to join the points together among themselves so that you get a pentagon with a five-pointed star inside it. Then the points of every star do not need to be joined.

Variation 2

Figure 103 shows a smaller dodecahedron inside a larger one. For this two complete dodecahedra are needed, the smaller being less than two thirds of the larger. It is a good idea either to paint the smaller dodecahedron with a little red transparent varnish to make it more visible or to take darker straws for the smaller star.

Place the smaller dodecahedron inside the larger one before the last two five-pointed stars are stuck together. Stick the thread joining the smaller dodecahedron to the larger ensuring that the distance between them is correct.

A straw ball

Materials
Straws
A sharp knife
Glue
A gold thread

Method
Iron the straws flat (see page 36) and cut them into strips about $1/8''$ (3 mm) wide. The ball in Figure 104 consists of eight rings. Because the rings are all stuck over each other the diameter of the innermost ring must be a fraction smaller

Figure 104. A straw ball.

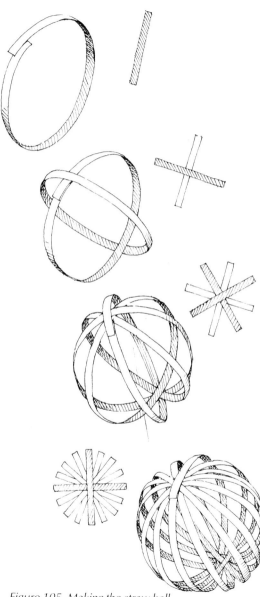

than that of the next one and so on. As the difference is scarcely perceptible the best way is to stick the two ends of the innermost ring with slightly more overlap than those of the next. Make the first two rings, allow them to dry fully and then stick them together in the form of a cross (Figure 105) making sure that the joints of the straws do not coincide exactly.

The glue of these rings stuck together must now dry fully because this is the foundation for the rest. Make the remaining six rings and allow them to dry too. Then fill up the gaps between the cross in the following way: begin by sticking two rings in the middle between the cross. Once this is quite dry stick the remaining four rings in the intervening spaces.

Allow the glue to dry properly, then glue a piece of thread on to one of the rings. The place where the thread is attached is important for the image produced by the ball: if it placed as in Figure 104 it produces the greatest effect of depth. The thread can, however, be attached to the cross-points of the rings so that the rings then give a vertical effect to the ball. If the thread is attached to the middle of a half ring this gives a horizontal effect. In this way one can create the impression that balls made in the same way are all different.

The balls can be easily damaged in storage. An extra ring placed at right angles round the other rings to keep the tension can offer some protection; one ring at right angles to another can also be the beginning of a whole series of variations. The breadth of the rings can also be varied; indeed one can place rings touching each other all the way round so that a true ball is formed.

Figure 105. Making the straw ball.

13. Constructions and models

The construction of a tetrahedron

Draw a line and mark on it points A and B. The distance AB determines the size of the tetrahedron. With a pair of compasses draw an arc radius AB, with A as a centre, above and below the line AB. Draw a second arc using B as a centre. The intersection of the arcs gives the points C and D. Join these points to A and B. Repeat this construction from A and D, and from B and D; this gives points E and F. Join these new points to the others and the tetrahedron is finished by drawing in the tabs for sticking (Figure 93 on page 71).

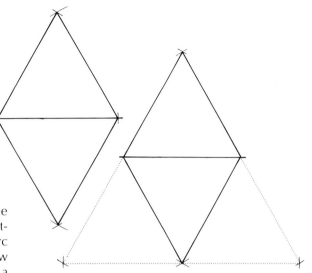

Figure 106. Constructing the tetrahedron.

The construction of a cube

With a pair of compasses, mark off points A, B, C, D and E at equal intervals along a line. The distance AB determines the size of the cube.

Draw arcs with radius AC from B and D to make point F and from C and E to make point G. From these two points draw vertical lines down to points C and D. Mark the distance CD from C twice on the vertical to find H and K, and similarly find J and L from D.

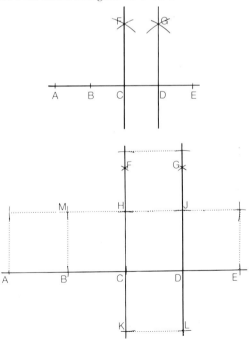

Figure 107. Constructing the cube. ▷

79

Draw a line through *H* and *J*, and through points *K* and *L*, thus forming three parallel lines. Mark distance *CD* off on the extension of line *HJ* to make points above *A*, *B* and *E*. Mark the same distance up the verticals above points *H* and *J*. Finally draw the tabs for sticking the cube together.

The construction of a pentagon

Draw a circle with compasses. Draw a horizontal line through the middle of the circle. Draw a vertical line crossing the horizontal line at the centre of the circle (Figure 108).

Find the centre of the line *AC* by cutting the circle at two points *D* and *E* with arcs of the radius of the circle and centre *A*. By joining *D* and *E* point *F* is obtained.

Mark the distance *FB* on the horizontal centre-line to give point *G*. The distance *BG* forms the length of the sides of the pentagon. With centre *B* mark this distance on the circle, to give points *H* and *I*. Mark the same distance off from *H* and *I* on the circle to give points *L* and *K*. The points *B, H, L, K* and *I* form the points of the pentagon.

This construction is not difficult but as an alternative the pattern opposite has been produced so that you can trace out an exact pentagon from one of the patterns without having to construct it.

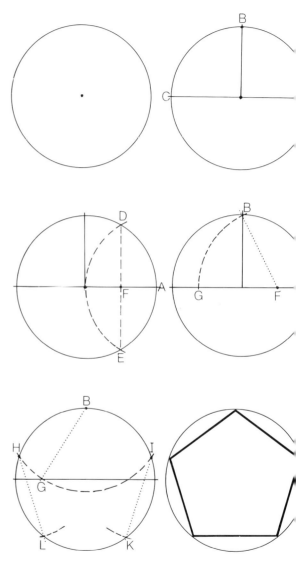

Figure 108. Constructing a pentagon.

80

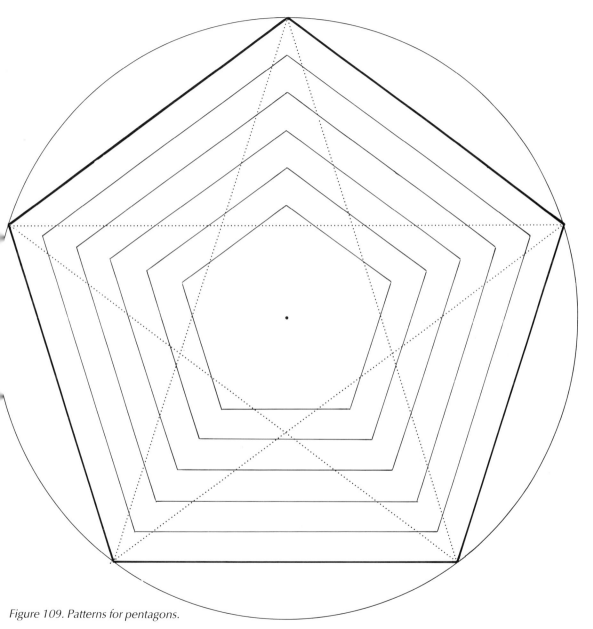

Figure 109. Patterns for pentagons.

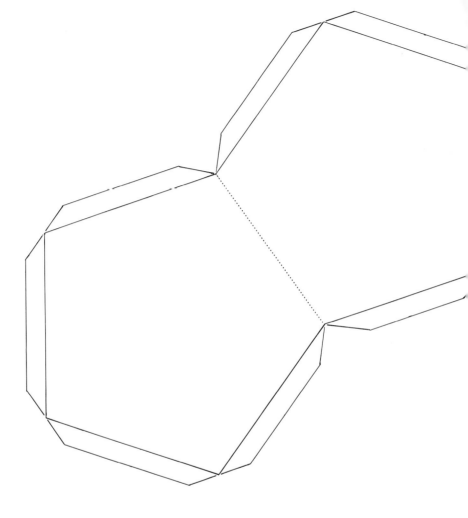

Figure 110. Pattern for a dodecahedron.

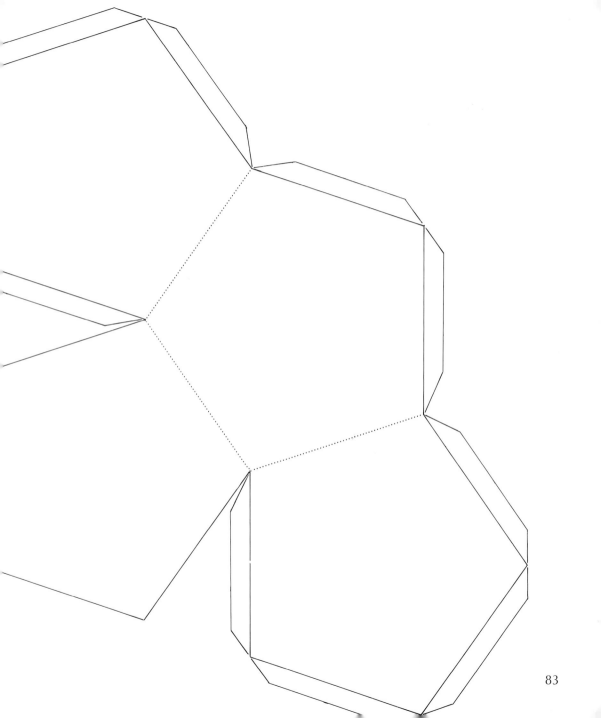

14. Materials

Usually one begins to think about making things for Christmas at the beginning of December but that can be too late for collecting certain natural objects. To decorate a door-wreath, an Advent wreath or the Christmas table-decoration with larch-cones or pine-cones, these must be col lected in autumn. The same applies to the wreath of pine-cones, for pine-cones in December are often rotted. The more one makes things from natural objects, the more aware one becomes of the natural world, and the easier it is to provide materials for Advent and Christmas creativity.

The materials for the Christmas decorations described in this book can usually be obtained in drawing and artist's materials shops, craft or model-building shops, office stationers, or do-it-yourself centres.

Greenery for Advent

Not everyone has a garden from which to collect the materials for Christmas and Advent creations. It may be possible to buy little sprigs at garden-centres or florists. Friends' gardens may yield hedge-cuttings or public gardens may have clippings. Clearance work in forestry areas or on building sites often produce large amounts of greenery. Do not leave it to the last moment and you should have no difficulty gathering material. Leave greenery outside in the shade. Obtaining greenery, fir or yew, for the Advent wreath is not easy. It is occasionally available for sale but expensive. It is better to get cut branches from forests in good time.

Paper and cardstock

Tissue-paper can be obtained in 15–20 colours. *Kite-paper (transparency paper)* is stronger than tissue-paper and has a shiny finish. It is obtainable in 6–8 colours. *Tracing paper* for making transparencies should not be too thin. It is available in pads (letter or A4 size) or from more specialist drawing suppliers in larger sizes and rolls.

Drawing-paper can be obtained in various weights in pads, or larger sizes in loose sheets from artist's materials shops. *White cardstock* should be strong: 300 gsm, 110 lb cover. Also needed are *dark blue cardstock* and thick *dark blue paper*.

Gold paper is a thin paper, gold on one side, while *gold and silver foil* is a thin metal foil which is gold-coloured on one side and silver-coloured on the other. (Also available are other combinations: gold/gold, gold/red, etc.)

Gold and silver cardstock is card with gold (or silver) on one side only.

Parchment or lampshade paper is a pliable card that has a kind of parchment or patterned stamp.

Adhesives

Water-based glue or *glue-sticks* can be used among other things for transparencies. They are effective for tissue-paper, but will come unstuck after a time on kite-paper (transparency paper) because this paper is not porous. The advantage of the glue-stick is that used sparingly it will not leave visible blobs. Remember to put the top back on to prevent it drying out.

Adhesives are available for many different purposes. Follow the instructions on the tubes. Some adhesives incline badly to stringing. For straw stars and other small areas it is best to look for an adhesive which has a fine nozzle.

Candles and beeswax

Candles are readily available. Sometimes cheap candles are made of little granules pressed together, coated with a smooth outer layer of wax. These candles are not suitable for decorating, because if you press them too hard while decorating, the outer layer breaks and the granules crumble. *Beeswax candles* are more difficult to find, often only obtainable in special shops.

Beeswax for dipping candles can be obtained in blocks of pure beeswax or in bags of flakes. Flakes melt much more quickly than the blocks.

Decorating candles can be done with blocks of Stockmar modelling beeswax or with thin sheets of Stockmar candle decorating wax. Break a bit off the blocks of modelling wax and knead it till it is warm, for only then can it be properly worked. Modelling wax is quite transparent in contrast to decorating waxes which have more opaque colours. Decorating wax is easy to use: the designs for the candle can be cut out.

Stockmar products can be obtained in some shops. They are distributed in the United States by HearthSong, PO Box B, Sebastopol, CA 95473; in Britain obtainable from Helios Fountain, 7 Grassmarket, Edinburgh EH1 2HY; in New Zealand from Ceres Enterprises, PO Box 11-336, Auckland.

Other materials

Teased unspun sheep's wool in long skeins can sometimes be bought in craft shops. If this is not possible, it may be necessary to buy a fleece and card the wool oneself. This is quite a lot of work, though very satisfying.

Straws. Some craft shops may have packets of thick and thin straws for craft work. If they cannot be found there, they must be obtained from a farmer at harvesting time. Cut the straw to avoid nodes in the lengths to be used for making stars. If the straws are to be cut open thick straws are needed.

Craft shops have *gold thread* and *silver filigree wire* (for making jewellery) in various gauges: $1/64$ ", $2/100$", $1/32$", $4/100$" (0.4 mm, 0.6 mm, 0.8 mm and 1 mm). For the mobile described in this book ⁴/₁₀₀" (0.6 mm) is suitable. If heavier objects are to be hung on the mobile it is better to take a heavier wire.

Wire for the frame of the Advent wreath should be from ¹/₁₆" to ¹/₈" (2 to 3 mm) thick, depending on the size of the wreath. For candle-holders use *thinner wire* ¹/₃₂" (0.9 mm). Garden centres or do-it-yourself shops stock wire.

Florist's flower blocks or oasis can be obtained in various sizes from florists or garden centres.

Finally, *pipe-cleaners* are obtainable in tobacconists and craft shops.